Jerry Thomas' Bartenders Guide: How to Mix Drinks 1862 Reprint: A Bon Vivant's Companion
By Jerry Thomas

Coming Soon
How I Stole 5.6 Million from Walmart
The Gods Return Loki's Trial
Zombie Squirrels

Loki's Publishing

http://www.facebook.com/LokisPublishing
Seattle, WA

How to Mix Drinks

Contents

PREFACE.

IN all ages of the world, and in all countries, men have indulged in "social drinks." They have always possessed themselves of some popular beverage apart from water and those of the breakfast and tea table. Whether it is judicious that mankind should continue to indulge in such things, or whether it would be wiser to abstain from all enjoyments of that character, it is not our province to decide. We leave that question to the moral philosopher. We simply contend that a relish for "social drinks" is universal; that those drinks exist in greater variety in the United States than in any other country in the world; and that he, therefore, who proposes to impart to these drinks not only the most palatable but the most wholesome characteristics of which they may be made susceptible, is a genuine public benefactor. That is exactly our object in introducing this little volume to the public. We do not propose to persuade any man to drink, for instance, a punch, or a julep, or a cocktail, who has never happened to make the acquaintance of those refreshing articles under circumstances calculated to induce more intimate relations; but we do propose to instruct those whose "intimate relations" in question render them somewhat fastidious, in the daintiest fashions thereunto pertaining. We very well remember seeing one day in London, in the rear of the Bank of England, a small drinking saloon that had been set up by a peripatetic American, at the door of which was placed a board covered with the unique titles of the American mixed drinks supposed to be prepared within that limited establishment. The "Connecticut eye-openers" and "Alabama fog-cutters," together with the "lightning-smashes" and the "thunderbolt-cocktails," created a profound sensation in the crowd assembled to peruse the Nectarian bill of fare, if they did not produce custom. It struck us, then, that a list of all the social drinks —the composite beverages, if we may call them so—of America, would really be one of the curiosities of jovial literature; and that if it was combined with a catalogue of the mixtures common to other nations, and made practically useful by the addition of a concise description of the various processes for "brewing" each, it would be a "blessing to mankind." There would be no excuse for imbibing, with such a book at hand, the "villainous compounds" of bar-keeping Goths and Vandals, who know no more of the amenities of bon vivant existence than a Hottentot can know of the bouquet of champagne.

Jerry Thomas

"There's philosophy," says Father Tom in the drama, "even in a jug of punch." We claim the credit of "philosophy teaching by example," then, to no ordinary extent in the composition of this volume; for our index exhibits the title of eighty-six different kinds of punches, together with a universe of cobblers, juleps, bitters, cups, slings, shrubs, &c, each and all of which the reader is carefully educated how to concoct in the choicest manner. For the perfection of this education, the name, alone, of Jerry Thomas is a sufficient guarantee. He has travelled Europe and America in search of all that is recondite in this branch of the spirit art. He has been the Jupiter Olympus of the bar at the Metropolitan Hotel in this city. He was the presiding deity at the Planter's House, St. Louis. He has been the proprietor of one of the most recherché saloons in New Orleans as well as in New York. His very name is synonymous in the lexicon of mixed drinks, with all that is rare and original. To the "Wine Press," edited by F. S. Cozzens, Esq., we are indebted for the composition of several valuable punches, and among them we may particularize the celebrated "Nuremburgh," and the equally famous "Philadelphia Fish House" punch. The rest we owe to the inspiration of Jerry Thomas himself, and as he is as inexorable as the Medes and Persians in his principle that no excellent drink can be made out of any thing but excellent materials, we conceive that we are safe in asserting that whatever may be prepared after his instructions will be able to speak eloquently for itself. "Good wine needs no bush," Shakespeare tells us and over one of Jerry's mixtures eulogy is quite as redundant. HOW TO MIX DRINKS; OR, THE BON-VIVANT'S COMPANION.

1. PUNCH.

To make punch of any sort in perfection, the ambrosial essence of the lemon must be extracted by rubbing lumps of sugar on the rind, which breaks the delicate little vessels that contain the essence, and at the same time absorbs it. This, and making the mixture sweet and strong, using tea instead of water, and thoroughly amalgamating all the compounds, so that the taste of neither the bitter, the sweet, the spirit, nor the element, shall be perceptible one over the other, is the grand secret, only to be acquired by practice.

In making hot toddy, or hot punch, you must put in the spirits before the water: in cold punch, grog, &c., the other way.

The precise portions of spirit and water, or even of the acidity and sweetness, can have no general rule, as scarcely two persons make punch alike.

2. Brandy Punch.

(Use large bar glass)

1 table-spoonful raspberry syrup.

2 do. white sugar.

1 wine-glass water,

1 1/2 do. brandy.

1/2 small-sized lemon.

2 slices of orange,

1 piece of pine-apple.

Fill the tumbler with shaved ice, shake well, and dress the top with berries in season; sip through a straw.

3. Brandy Punch.

(For a party of twenty.)

1 gallon of water.

3 quarts of brandy.

1/2 pint of Jamaica rum.

2 lbs. of sugar.

Juice of 6 lemons.

3 oranges sliced.

Jerry Thomas

1 pine-apple, pared, and cut up.

1 gill of Curaçoa. {Approximately 4 ounces}

2 gills of raspberry syrup.

Ice, and add berries in season.

Mix the materials well together in a large bowl, and you have a splendid punch.

4. Mississippi Punch.

(Use large bar glass.)

1 wine-glass of brandy.

1/2 do. Jamaica rum.

1/2 do. Bourbon whiskey.

1/2 do. water.

1 1/2 table-spoonful of powdered white sugar.

1/4 of a large lemon.

Fill a tumbler with shaved ice.

The above must be well shaken, and to those who like their draughts "like linked sweetness long drawn out," let them use a glass tube or straw to sip the nectar through. The top of this punch should be ornamented with small pieces of orange, and berries in season.

5. Hot Brandy and Rum Punch.

(For a party of fifteen.)

1 quart of Jamaica rum.

1 do. Cognac brandy.

1 lb. of white loaf-sugar.

4 lemons.

3 quarts of boiling water.

1 teaspoonful of nutmeg.

Rub the sugar over the lemons until it has absorbed all the yellow part of the skins, then put the sugar into a punch-bowl; add the ingredients well together, pour over them the boiling water, stir well together; add the rum, brandy and nutmeg; mix thoroughly, and the punch will be ready to serve. As we have before said, it is very important, in making good punch, that all the ingredients are thoroughly incorporated; and, to insure success, the process of mixing must be diligently attended to. Allow a quart for four persons; but this information must be taken cum grano salts; for the capacities of persons for this kind of beverage are generally supposed to vary considerably.

6. Irish Whiskey Punch.

This is the genuine Irish beverage. It is generally made one-third pure whiskey, two-thirds boiling water, in which the sugar has been dissolved. If lemon punch, the rind is rubbed on the sugar, and a small proportion of juice added before the whiskey is poured in.

7. Cold Whiskey Punch.

(For a party.)

This beverage ought always to be made with boiling water, and allowed to concoct and cool for a day or two before it is put on the table. In this way, the materials get more intensely amalgamated than cold water and cold whiskey ever get. As to the beautiful mutual adaptation of cold rum and cold water, that is beyond all praise, being one of Nature's most exquisite achievements. (See " Glasgow Punchy No. 29.) * Irish whiskey is not fit to drink until it is three years old. The best whiskey for this purpose is Kenahan's LL whiskey.

8. Scotch Whiskey Punch.

Steep the thin yellow shavings of lemon peel in the whiskey, which should be Glenlivet or Islay, of the best quality; the sugar should be dissolved in boiling water. As it requires genius to make whiskey punch, it would be impertinent to give proportions. (See "Spread Eagle Punch," No. 39.)

9. Whiskey Punch.

(Use small bar glass)

1 wine-glass whiskey (Irish or Scotch).

2 do. boiling water.

Sugar to taste.

Dissolve the sugar well with 1 wine-glass of the water, then pour in the whiskey, and add the balance of the water, sweeten to taste, and put in a small piece of lemon rind, or a thin slice of lemon.

10. Gin Punch.

(Use large bar glass.)
1 table-spoonful of raspberry syrup.
2 do. do. white sugar.
1 wine-glass of water.
1 1/2 do. gin.
1/2 small-sized lemon.
2 slices of orange.
1 piece of pine-apple.

Fill the tumbler with shaved ice. Shake well, and ornament the top with berries in season. Sip through a glass tube or straw.

11. Gin Punch.

(From a recipe by Soyer.)
1/2 pint of old gin.
1 gill of maraschino.
The juice of two lemons.
The rind of half a lemon.
Four ounces of syrup.
1 quart bottle of German Seltzer water.
Ice well.

12. Champagne Punch,

(Per bottle.)
1 quart bottle of wine,
1/4 lb. of sugar.
1 orange sliced.
The juice of a lemon.
3 slices of pine apple.

1 wine-glass of raspberry or strawberry syrup.

Ornament with fruits in season, and serve in champagne goblets.
This can be made in any quantity by observing the proportions of the ingredients as given above. Four bottles of wine make a gallon, and a gallon is generally sufficient for fifteen persons in a mixed party. For a good champagne punch, see "Rocky Mountain Punch" No. 43.

13. Sherry Punch.

(Use large bar glass.)

2 wine-glasses of sherry.

1 table-spoonful of sugar.

2 or 3 slices of orange.

2 do. do. lemon.

Fill tumbler with shaved ice, shake well, and ornament with berries in season. Sip through a straw.

14. Claret Punch.

(Use large bar glass.)

1 1/2 table-spoonful of sugar.

1 slice of lemon.

2 or 3 do. orange.

Fill the tumbler with shaved ice, and then pour in your claret, shake well, and ornament with berries in season. Place a straw in the glass. To make a quantity of claret punch, see "Imperial Punch" No. 41.

15. Sauterne Punch.

(Use large bar glass.)

The same as claret punch, using Sauterne instead of claret.

16. Port Wine Punch.

(Use large bar glass.)

The same as claret punch, using port wine instead of claret, and ornament with berries in season.

17. Vanilla Punch.

(Use large bar glass.)

1 table-spoonful of sugar.

1 wine-glass of brandy.

The juice of 1/4 of a lemon. Fill the tumbler with shaved ice, shake well, ornament with one or two slices of lemon, and flavor with a few drops of vanilla extract. This is a delicious drink, and should be imbibed through a glass tube or straw.

18. Pine-Apple Punch.

(For a party of ten.)

4 bottles of champagne.

1 pint of Jamaica rum.

1 do. brandy.

1 gill of Curaçoa.

Juice of 4 lemons.

4 pine-apples sliced.

Sweeten to taste with pulverized white sugar.

Put the pine-apple with one pound of sugar in a glass bowl, and let them stand until the sugar is well soaked in the pine-apple, then add all the other ingredients, except the champagne. Let this mixture stand in ice for about an hour, then add the champagne. Place a large block of ice in the centre of the bowl, and ornament it with loaf sugar, sliced orange, and other fruits in season. Serve in champagne glasses. Pine-apple punch is sometimes made by adding sliced pine-apple to brandy punch.

19. Orgeat Punch.

(Use large bar glass.)

1 1/2 table-spoonful of orgeat syrup.

1 1/2 wine-glass of brandy.

Juice of a lemon, and fill the tumbler with shaved ice. Shake well, ornament with berries in season, and dash port wine on top.

Place the straw, as represented in cut of mint julep.

20. Curaçoa Punch.

(Use large bar glass.)

1 table spoonful of sugar.

1 wine-glass of brandy.

1/2 do. do. Jamaica rum.

1 do. do. water.

1/2 pony glass of Curaçoa.

The juice of half a lemon.

Fill the tumbler with shaved ice, shake well, and ornament with fruits of the season; sip the nectar through a straw.

21. Roman Punch.

(Use large bar glass.)

1 table-spoonful of sugar.

1 do.   do. raspberry syrup.

1 tea-spoonful of Curaçoa.

1 wine-glass of Jamaica rum.

1/2 do. do. brandy.

The juice of half a lemon.

Fill with shaved ice, shake well, dash with port wine, and ornament with fruits in season. Imbibe through a straw.

22. Milk Punch.

(Use large bar glass.)

1 table-spoonful of fine white sugar.

2 do. water.

1 wine-glass of Cognac brandy.

1/2 do. Santa Cruz rum.

1/3 Tumblerful of shaved ice. Fill with milk, shake the ingredients well together, and grate a little nutmeg on top.

23. Hot Milk Punch.

(Use large bar glass.)

This punch is made the same as the above, with the exception that hot milk is used, and no ice.

24. English Milk Punch.

Put the following ingredients into a very clean pitcher, viz.:
The juice of six lemons.
The rind of two do.
1 lb. of sugar.
1 pine-apple, peeled, sliced and pounded.
6 cloves.
20 coriander seeds.
1 small stick of cinnamon.
1 pint of brandy. 1 do rum.
*1 gill of arrack.
1 cup of strong green tea.
1 quart of boiling water.
The boiling water to be added last; cork this down to prevent evaporation, and allow these ingredients to steep for at least six hours; then add a quart of hot milk and the juice of two lemons; mix, and filter through a jelly bag; and when the punch has passed bright, put it away in tight-corked bottles.
This punch is intended to be iced for drinking.

25. English Milk Punch.

(Another method.)
This seductive and nectareous drink can also be made by the directions herewith given:
To two quarts of water add one quart of milk. Mix one quart of old Jamaica rum with two of French brandy, and put the spirit to the milk, stirring it for a short time; let it stand for an hour, but do not suffer any one of delicate appetite to see the melange in its present state, as the sight might create a distaste for the punch when perfected. Filter through blotting-paper into bottles; and should you find that the liquid is cloudy, which it should not be, you may clarify it by adding a small portion of isinglass to each bottle. The above receipt will furnish you with half a dozen of punch.

26. Punch à la Ford.

(A recipe from Benson E. Hill, Esq, author of The Epicure's Almanac.)
The late General Ford, who for many years was the commanding engineer
at Dover, kept a most hospitable board, and used to make punch on a large
scale, after the following method:

He would select three dozen of lemons, the coats of which were smooth,
and whose rinds were not too thin; these he would peel with a sharp knife
into a large earthen vessel, taking care that none of the rind should be
detached but that portion in which the cells are placed, containing the
essential oil; when he had completed the first part of the process, he added
two pounds of lump-sugar, and stirred the peel and sugar together with an
oar-shaped piece of wood, for nearly half an hour, thereby extracting a
greater quantity of the essential oil. Boiling water was next poured into the
vessel, and the whole well stirred, until the sugar was completely
dissolved. The lemons were then cut and squeezed, the juice strained from
the kernels; these were placed in a separate jug, and boiling water poured
upon them, the general being aware that the pips were enveloped in a thick
mucilage, full of flavor; half the lemon juice was now thrown in; and as
soon as the kernels were free from their transparent coating, their liquor
was strained and added.

The sherbet was now tasted; more acid or more sugar applied as required,
and care taken not to render the lemonade too watery. "Rich of the fruit,
and plenty of sweetness," was the general's maxim. The sherbet was then
measured, and to every three quarts a pint of Cognac brandy and a pint of
old Jamaica rum were allotted, the spirit being well stirred as poured in;
bottling immediately followed, and, when completed, the beverage was
kept in a cold cellar, or tank, till required. At the general's table I have
frequently drunk punch thus made, more than six months old; and found it
much improved by time and a cool atmosphere.

27. Punch Jelly.

Make a good bowl of punch, a la Ford, already described. To every pint of
punch add an ounce and a half of isinglass, dissolved in a quarter of a pint

of water (about half a tumbler full); pour this into the punch whilst quite hot, and then fill your moulds, taking care that they are not disturbed until the jelly is completely set.

Orange, lemon, or calf s-foot jelly, not used at dinner, can be converted into punch jelly for the evening, by following the above directions, only taking care to omit a portion of the acid prescribed in making the sherbet.

This preparation is a very agreeable refreshment on a cold night, but should be used in moderation; the strength of the punch is so artfully concealed by its admixture with the gelatine, that many persons, particularly of the softer sex, have been tempted to partake so plentifully of it as to render them somewhat unfit for waltzing or quadrilling after supper.

28. Gin Punch.

(For bottling.)

Following General Ford's plan, as already described, for making sherbet, add good gin, in the proper proportion before prescribed; this, bottled and kept in a cool cellar or cistern, will be found an economical and excellent summer drink.

29. Glasgow Punch.

(From a recipe in the possession of Dr. Shelton Mackenzie.)

Melt lump-sugar in cold water, with the juice of a couple of lemons, passed through a fine hair-strainer. This is sherbet, and must be well mingled. Then add old Jamaica rum—one part of rum to five of sherbet. Cut a couple of limes in two, and run each section rapidly around the edge of the jug or bowl, gently squeezing in some of the delicate acid. This done, the punch is made. Imbibe.

30. Regent's Punch.

(For a party of twenty.)

The ingredients for this renowned panels are:—

3 bottles champagne.

1 do. Hockheimer.

How to Mix Drinks
1 do. Curaçoa.
1 do. Cognac.
1/2 do. Jamaica rum.
2 do. Madeira.
2 do. Seltzer, or plain soda-water.
4 lbs. bloom raisins.
To which add oranges, lemons, rock candy, and instead of water, green tea to taste. Refrigerate with all the icy power of the Arctic.

31. Regent's Punch.

(Another recipe.)
(From the Bordeaux Wine and Liquor Guide.)
1 1/2 pint, each, strong hot green tea, lemon juice, and capillaire.*
1 pint, each, rum, brandy, arrack, and Curaçoa.
1 bottle of champagne; mix, and slice a pine-apple into it
For still another method of compounding this celebrated punch, see recipe No. 295, in "The Manual for the Manufacture of Cordials, etc." in the latter part of this work.

32. Raspberry Punch.

(From a recipe in the Bordeaux Wine and Liquor Guide.)
1 1/2 gill of raspberry juice, or vinegar.
3/4 lb. lump-sugar.
3 1/2 pints of boiling water.
Infuse half an hour, strain, add 1 pint of porter, J to 1 pint, each, of rum and brandy (or either 14 to 2 pints), and add more warm water and sugar, if desired weaker or sweeter. A liqueur of glass of Curaçoa, noyau, or maraschino, improves it.

33. National Guard 7th Regiment Punch.

(Use large bar glass.)
1 table-spoonful of sugar.
The juice of a 1/4 of a lemon.
1 wine-glass of brandy.

1 do. do. Catawba wine.

Flavor with raspberry syrup.

Fill the glass with shaved ice. Shake and mix thoroughly then ornament with slices of orange, pineapple, and berries in season, and dash with Jamaica rum. This delicious beverage should be imbibed through a straw.

* See recipes Nos. 65 and 66.

34. St. Charles' Punch.

(Use large bar glass.)

1 table-spoonful of sugar.

1 wine-glass of port wine.

1 pony do. brandy.

The juice of 1/4 of a lemon.

Fill the tumbler with shaved ice, shake well, and ornament with fruits in season, and serve with a straw.

35. 69th Regiment Punch.

(In earthen mug.)

1/2 wine-glass of Irish whiskey.

1/2 do. do. Scotch do.

1 tea-spoonful of sugar.

1 piece of lemon.

2 wine-glasses of hot water.

This is a capital punch for a cold night.

36. Louisiana Sugar-House Punch.

(From a recipe in the possession of Colonel T B. Thorpe.)

To one quart of boiling syrup, taken from the kettles, add whiskey or brandy to suit the "patient." Flavor with the juice of sour oranges.

37. Dry Punch.

(From a recipe by Santina, the celebrated Spanish caterer.)

2 gallons of brandy.

1 do. water.

1/2 do. tea.
1 pint of Jamaica rum.
1/2 do. Curaçoa.
Juice of six lemons.
1 1/2 lb. white sugar.

Mix thoroughly, and strain, as already described in the recipe for "Punch à la Ford," adding more sugar and lemon juice, if to taste. Bottle, and keep on ice for three or four days, and the punch will be ready for use, but the longer it stands, the better it gets.

38. La Patria Punch.

(For a party of twenty.)
(From a recipe in the possession of H. P. Leland, Esq.)
3 bottles of champagne, iced.
1 bottle of Cognac.
6 oranges.
1 pineapple.

Slice the oranges and pineapples in a bowl, pour the cognac over them, and let them steep for a couple of hours, then in with the champagne and serve immediately.

39. The Spread Eagle Punch.

1 bottle of Islay whiskey.
1 bottle Monongahela, Lemon peel, sugar and—boiling water at discretion.

40. Rochester Punch.

(For a party of twenty.)
(From a recipe in the possession of Boswell Hart, Esq.)
2 bottles of sparkling Catawba.
2 do. do. Isabella.
1 do. Sauterne.
2 wine glasses of maraschino.
2 do. do. Curaçoa.

Jerry Thomas

Fill the tranquil bowl with ripe strawberries. Should the strawberry season be over, or under, add a few drops of extract of peach or vanilla.

41. Imperial Punch.

1 bottle of claret.

1 do. soda-water.

4 table-spoonfuls of powdered white sugar.

1/4 teaspoonful of grated nutmeg.

1 liqueur glass of maraschino.

About lb. of ice. 3 or 4 slices of cucumber rind.

Put all the ingredients into a bowl or pitcher and mix well.

42. Thirty-Second Regiment or Victoria Punch.

(For a party of twenty.)

(Receipts from the late Wm. H. Herbert, Esq.)

6 lemons, in slices.

1/2 gallon of brandy.

1/2 do. Jamaica rum.

1 lb. of white sugar.

1 3/4 quart of water.

1 pint of "boiling milk.

Steep the lemons for twenty-four hours in the brandy and rum; add the sugar, water and milk, and when well mixed, strain through a jelly-bag.

This punch may be bottled, and used afterward hot or cold.

Half the above quantity, or even less, may be made, as this recipe is for a party of twenty.

43. Rocky Mountain Punch.

(For a mixed party of twenty.)

(From a recipe in the possession of Major James Foster.)

This delicious punch is compounded as follows:

5 bottles of champagne.

1 quart of Jamaica rum.

1 pint of maraschino.

6 lemons, sliced.

Sugar to taste.

Mix the above ingredients in a large punch-bowl, then place in the centre of the bowl a large square block of ice, ornamented on top with rock candy, loaf-sugar, sliced lemons or oranges, and fruits in season. This is a splendid punch for New Year's Day.

44. Punch Grassot.

(The following recipe was given by M. Grassot, the eminent French comedian of the Palais Royal, to Mr. Howard Paul, the celebrated "Entertainer," when performing in Paris.)

1 wine-glass of brandy.

5 drops of Curaçoa.

1 do. acetic acid.

2 teaspoonfuls of simple syrup.

1 teaspoonful of syrup of strawberries.

1/4 of a pint of water.

The peel of a small lemon, sliced.

Mix, serve up with ice, in large goblet, and, if possible, garnish the top with a slice of peach or apricot. In cold weather this punch is admirable served hot.

45. Light Guard Punch.

(For a party of twenty.)

3 bottles of champagne.

1 do. pale sherry.

1 do. Cognac.

1 do. Sauterne.

1 pineapple, sliced.

4 lemons, do Sweeten to taste, mix in a punch-bowl, cool with a large lump of ice, and serve immediately.

46. Philadelphia Fish-House Punch.

(From a recipe In the possession of Charles G. Leland, Esq.)

Jerry Thomas
1/3 pint of lemon juice.
3/4 lb. of white sugar.
1 pint of mixture.*
2 1/2 pints of cold water.
The above is generally sufficient for one person.

47. Non-Such Punch.

6 bottles of claret.
6 do. soda-water.
1 do. brandy.
1 do. sherry,
1/2 pint of green tea.
Juice of three lemons.
1/2 of a pineapple cut up in small pieces.
Sweeten with white sugar to taste. Strain a bottle immediately. Keep for one month before using.
* To make this mixture, take pint of peach brandy, pint of Cognac brandy, and pint of Jamaica rum.
This is a delicious and safe drink for a mixed evening party. Cool before serving.

48. Canadian Punch.

2 quarts of rye whiskey.
1 pint of Jamaica rum.
6 lemons, sliced,
1 pineapple, do.
4 quarts of water.
Sweeten to taste, and ice.

49. Tip-Top Punch.
(For a party of five.)
1 bottle of champagne.
2 do. soda-water.
1 liqueur glass of Curaçoa.
2 table-spoonfuls of powdered sugar.

1 slice of pineapple, cut up.
Put all the ingredients together in a small punch-bowl, mix well, and serve in champagne goblets.

50. Arrack.

Most of the arrack imported into this country is distilled from rice, and comes from Batavia. It is but little used in America, except to flavor punch; the taste of it is very agreeable in this mixture. Arrack improves very much with age. It is much used in some parts of India, where it is distilled from toddy, the juice of the cocoanut tree. An imitation of arrack punch is made by adding to a bowl of punch a few grains of benzoin, commonly called flowers of Benjamin. See recipe No. 36, in "The Manual for the Manufacture of Cordials, etc.," in the end of this volume.

51. Arrack Punch.

In making 'rack punch, you ought to put two glasses (wine-glasses) of rum to three of arrack. A good deal of sugar is required; but sweetening, after all, must be left to taste. Lemons and limes are also matter of palate, but two lemons are enough for the above quantity; put then an equal quantity of water—i. e., not five but six glasses to allow for the lemon juice, and you have a very pretty three tumblers of punch.

52. Arrack Punch.

(Another method.)
Steep in one quart of old Batavia arrack, six lemons cut in thin slices, for six hours. At the end of that time the lemon must be removed without squeezing. Dissolve one pound of loaf-sugar in one quart of boiling water, and add the hot solution to the arrack. Let it stand to cool. This is a delightful liqueur, and should be used as such. See recipe No. 342, in "The Manual for the Manufacture of Cordials, etc.," in the end of this volume.

53. Bimbo Punch. Bimbo is made nearly in the same way as the above, except that Cognac brandy is substituted for arrack.

54. Cold Punch. Arrack, port wine and water, of each two pints, one pound of loaf-sugar, and the juice of eight lemons.

55. Nuremburgh Punch.

(For a party of fifteen.)

(From a recipe in the possession of Hon. Gulian C. Verplanck.)

Take three-quarters of a pound of loaf-sugar, press upon it, through muslin, the juice of two or more good sized oranges; add a little of the peel, cut very thin, pour upon a quart of boiling water, the third part of that quantity of Batavia arrack, and a bottle of hot, but not boiling, red or white French wine—red is best. Stir together. This is excellent when cold, and will improve by age.

56. United Service Punch.

Dissolve, in two pints of hot tea, three-quarters of a pound of loaf-sugar, having previously rubbed off, with a portion of the sugar, the peel of four lemons; then add the juice of eight lemons, and a pint of arrack.

57. Ruby Punch.

Dissolve, in three pints of hot tea, one pound of sugar; add thereto the juice of six lemons, a pint of arrack, and a pint of port wine.

58. Royal Punch.

1 pint of hot green tea.

1/2 do. brandy.

1/2 do. Jamaica rum.

1 wine-glass of Curaçoa.

1 do. do. arrack.

Juice of two limes.

A thin slice of lemon.

White sugar to taste.

1 gill of warm calf's-foot jelly.

To be drunk as hot as possible.

This is a composition worthy of a king, and the materials are admirably blended; the inebriating effects of the spirits being deadened by the tea, whilst the jelly softens the mixture, and destroys the acrimony of the acid and sugar. The whites of a couple of eggs well beat up to a froth, may be substituted for the jelly where that is not at hand. If the punch is too strong, add more green tea to taste.

59. Century Club Punch.

Two parts old St. Cruz rum; one part old Jamaica rum, five parts water; lemons and sugar ad lib. This is a nice punch.

60. Duke of Norfolk Punch.

In twenty quarts of French brandy put the peels of thirty lemons and thirty oranges, pared so thin that not the least of the white is left. Infuse twelve hours. Have ready thirty quarts of cold water that has boiled; put to it fifteen pounds of double-refined sugar; and when well mixed, pour it upon the brandy and peels, adding the juice of the oranges and of twenty-four lemons; mix well, then strain through a very fine hair-sieve, into a very clean barrel that has held spirits, and put in two quarts of new milk. Stir, and then bung it close; let it stand six weeks in a warm cellar; bottle the liquor for use, observing great care that the bottles are perfectly clean and dry, and the corks of the best quality, and well put in. This liquor will keep many years, and improve by age.

(Another way.)

Pare six lemons and three oranges very thin, squeeze the juice into a large teapot, put to it two quarts of brandy, one of white wine, and one of milk, and one pound and a quarter of sugar. Let it be mixed, and then covered for twenty-four hours, strain through a jelly-bag till clear, then bottle it.

61. Queen Punch.

Put two ounces of cream of tartar, and the juice and parings of two lemons, into a stone jar; pour on them seven quarts of boiling water, stir and cover close. When cold, sweeten with loaf-sugar, and straining it, bottle and cork it tight. This is a very pleasant liquor, and very wholesome; but from the latter consideration was at one time drank in such quantities as to become injurious. Add, in bottling, half a pint of rum to the whole quantity.

62. Gothic Punch.

(For a party of ten.)

(From a recipe in the possession of Bayard Taylor, Esq.)

Four bottles still Catawba; one bottle claret, three oranges, or one pineapple, ten table-spoonfuls of sugar. Let this mixture stand in a very cold place, or in ice, for one hour or more, then add one bottle of champagne.

63. Oxford Punch.

We have been favored by an English gentleman with the following recipe for the concoction of punch as drunk by the students of the University of Oxford:

Rub the rinds of three fresh lemons with loaf-sugar till you have extracted a portion of the juice; cut the peel finely off two lemons more, and two sweet oranges. Use the juice of six lemons, and four sweet oranges. Add six glasses of calf's-foot jelly; let all be put into a large jug, and stir well together. Pour in two quarts of water boiling hot, and set the jug upon the hob for twenty minutes. Strain the liquor through a fine sieve into a large bowl; pour in a bottle of capillaire,* half a pint of sherry, a pint of Cognac brandy, a pint of old Jamaica rum, and a quart of orange shrub; stir well as you pour in the spirit. If you find it requires more sweetness, add sugar to your taste.

64. Uncle Toby Punch. (English.)

Take two large fresh lemons with rough skins, quite ripe, and some large lumps of double-refined sugar. Rub the sugar over the lemons till it has absorbed all the yellow part of the skins. Then put into the bowl these lumps, and as much more as the juice of the lemons may be supposed to require; for no certain weight can be mentioned, as the acidity of a lemon cannot be known till tried, and therefore this must be determined by the taste. Then squeeze the lemon juice upon the sugar; and, with a bruiser press the sugar and the juice particularly well together, for a great deal of the richness and fine flavor of the punch depends on this rubbing and mixing process being thoroughly performed. Then mix this up very well with boiling water (soft water is best) till the whole is rather cool. When this mixture (which is now called the sherbet) is to your taste, take brandy and rum in equal quantities, and put them to it, mixing the whole well together again. The quantity of liquor must be according to your taste; two good lemons are generally enough to make four quarts of punch, including a quart of liquor, with half a pound of sugar; but this depends much on taste, and on the strength of the spirit.

* 65. Capillaire.—Put a wine-glass of Curaçoa into a pint of clarified syrup, shake them well together, and pour it into the proper sized bottles. A tea-spoonful in a glass of fair water makes a pleasant eau sucré, see No. 346 "Manual for the Manufacture of Cordials, etc.," at the end of this book.

66. Another recipe for making Capillaire

.—To one gallon of water add twenty-eight pounds of loaf-sugar; put both over the fire to simmer; when milk-warm add the whites of four or five eggs, well beaten; as these simmer with tho syrup, skim it well; then pour it off, and flavor it with orange flower water or bitter almonds, whichever you prefer. As the pulp is disagreeable to some persons, the sherbet may be strained before the liquor is put in. Some strain the lemon before they put it' to the sugar, which is improper, as, when the pulp and sugar are well mixed together, it adds much to the richness of the punch.

When only rum is used, about half a pint of porter will soften the punch; and even when both rum and brandy are used, the porter gives a richness, and to some a very pleasant flavor.

67. Punch a la Romaine.

(For a party of fifteen.)

Take the juice of ten lemons and two sweet oranges, dissolve in it two pounds of powdered sugar, and add the thin rind of an orange, run this through a sieve, and stir in by degrees the whites of ten eggs, beaten into a froth. Put the bowl with the mixture into an ice pail, let it freeze a little,

then stir briskly into it a bottle of wine and a bottle of rum. For another
method of making this punch, see recipe No. 296 in "The Manual for the
Manufacture of Cordials, etc." in the latter part of this work.

68. Tea Punch.

Make an infusion of the best green tea, an ounce to a quart of boiling
water; put before the fire a silver or other metal bowl, to become quite hot,
and then put into it
1/2 pint of good brandy.
1/2 do. rum.
1/4 lb. of lump-sugar.
The juice of a large lemon.
Set these a-light, and pour in the tea gradually, mixing it from time to time
with a ladle; it will remain burning for some time, and is to be poured in
that state into the "glasses ; in order to increase the flavor, a few lumps of
the sugar should be rubbed over the lemon peel. This punch may be made
in a china bowl, but in that case the flame goes off more rapidly.

69. West Indian Punch.

This punch is made the same as brandy punch, but to each glass add a
clove or two of preserved ginger, and a little of the syrup.

70. Barbadoes Punch.

To each glass of brandy punch, add a table-spoonful of guava jelly.

71. Yorkshire Punch.

Rub off the rind of three lemons on pieces of sugar, put the sugar into a
jug, and add to it the thin rind of one lemon and an orange, and the juice of
four oranges and often lemons, with six glasses of dissolved calf's-foot
jelly. Pour two quarts of water over the whole, mixing the materials well,
then cover the jug, and keep it on a warm hearth for twenty minutes. Then
strain the mixture, and add a pint of clarified syrup, half a pint each of rum
and brandy, and a bottle of good orange or lemon shrub.

72. Apple Punch.

Lay in a china bowl slices of apples and lemons alternately, each layer being thickly strewed with powdered sugar. Pour over the fruit, when the bowl is half filled, a bottle of claret; cover, and let it stand six hours. Then pour it through a muslin bag, and send it up immediately.

73. Ale Punch.

A quart of mild ale, a glass of white wine, one of brandy, one of capillaire, the juice of a lemon, a roll of the peel pared thin, nutmeg grated on the top, and a bit of toasted bread.

74. Cider Punch.

On the thin rind of half a lemon pour half a pint of sherry; add a quarter of a pound of sugar, the juice of a lemon, a little grated nutmeg, and a bottle of cider; mix it well, and, if possible, place it in ice. Add, before sent in, a glass of brandy, and a few pieces of cucumber rind.

75. Nectar Punch.

Infuse the peel of fifteen lemons in a pint and a half of rum for forty-eight hours, add two quarts of cold water with three pints of rum, exclusive of the pint and a half; also the juice of the lemons, with two quarts of boiling-hot milk, and one grated nutmeg; pour the milk on the above, and let it stand twenty-four hours, covered close; add two pounds and a half of loaf-sugar; then strain it through a flannel bag. till quite fine, and bottle it for use. It is fit to use as soon as bottled.

76. Orange Punch.

From a recipe in the "Bordeaux Wine and Liquor Guide."
The juice of 3 or 4 oranges.
The peel of 1 or 2 do.
3/4 lb. lump-sugar.
3 1/2 pints of boiling water.

Infuse half an hour, strain, add 1/2 pint of porter; 3/4 to 1 pint each, rum and brandy (or either alone 1 1/2 to 2 pints), and add more warm water and sugar, if desired weaker or sweeter. A liqueur glass of Curaçoa, noyau, or maraschino improves it. A good lemon punch may be made by substituting lemons instead of oranges.

77. Imperial Raspberry Whiskey Punch,

For the recipe to make this punch, see No. 292 in " The Manual for the Manufacture of Cordials, etc." in the end of this work. This recipe is for 10 gallons.

78. Kirschwasser Punch.

See recipe No. 293, in "The Manual for the Manufacture of Cordials, etc." in the latter part of this book. This recipe is for 10 gallons.

79. D'Orsay Punch.

See recipe No. 294 in " The Manual for the Manufacture of Cordials, etc." in the latter part of this book. This recipe is for 10 gallons.

80. EGG NOGG.

Egg Nogg is a beverage of American origin, but it has a popularity that is cosmopolitan. At the South it is almost indispensable at Christmas time, and at the North it is a favorite at all seasons.

In Scotland they call Egg Nogg, " auld man's milk."

81. Egg Nogg.

(Use large bar glass.)

1 table-spoonful of fine sugar, dissolved with

1 do. cold water,

1 egg.

1 wine-glass of Cognac brandy.

1/2 do. Santa Cruz rum.

1/3 tumblerful of milk.

Fill the tumbler 1/4 full with shaved ice, shake the ingredients until they are thoroughly mixed together, and grate a little nutmeg on top. Every well ordered bar has a tin egg-nogg "shaker," which is a great aid in mixing this beverage.

82. Hot Egg Nogg.

(Use large bar glass)

This drink is very popular in California, and is made in precisely the same manner as the cold egg nogg above, except that you must use boiling water instead of ice.

83. Egg Nogg.

(For a party of forty.)

1 dozen eggs.

2 quarts of brandy.

1 pint of Santa Cruz rum.

2 gallons of milk.

1 1/2 lbs. white sugar.

Separate the whites of the eggs from the yolks, beat them separately with an egg-beater until the yolks are well cut up, and the whites assume a light fleecy appearance. Mix all the ingredients (except the whites of the eggs) in a large punch bowl, then let the whites float on top, and ornament with colored sugars. Cool in a tub of ice, and serve.

84. Baltimore Egg Nogg.

(For a party of fifteen.)

Take the yellow of sixteen eggs and twelve table-spoonfuls of pulverized loaf-sugar, and beat them to the consistence of cream; to this add two-thirds of a nutmeg grated, and beat well together; then mix in half a pint of good brandy or Jamaica rum, and two wine-glasses of Madeira wine. Have ready the whites of the eggs, beaten to a stiff froth, and beat them into the above-described mixture. When this is all done, stir in six pints of good rich milk. There is no heat used. Egg Nogg made in this manner is digestible, and will not cause headache. It makes an excellent drink for debilitated persons, and a nourishing diet for consumptives.

85. General Harrison's Egg Nogg,

(Use large bar glass.)

1 egg. teaspoonful of sugar.

2 or 3 small lumps of ice.

Fill the tumbler with cider, and shake well.

This is a splendid drink, and is very popular on the Mississippi river. It was General Harrison's favorite beverage.

86. Sherry Egg Nogg.

1 table-spoonful of white sugar.

1 egg.

2 wine-glasses of sherry.

Dissolve the sugar with a little water; break the yolk of the egg in a large glass; put in one-quarter tumblerful of broken ice; fill with milk, and shake up until the egg is thoroughly mixed with the other ingredients, then grate a little nutmeg on top, and quaff the nectar cup.

87. JULEPS.

The julep is peculiarly an American beverage, and in the Southern states is more popular than any other. It was introduced into England by Captain Marryatt, where it is now quite a favorite. The gallant captain seems to have had a penchant for the nectareous drink, and published the recipe in his work on America. We give it in his own words: "I must descant a little upon the mint julep, as it is, with the thermometer at 100°, one of the most delightful and insinuating potations that ever was invented, and may be drunk with equal satisfaction when the thermometer is as low as 70°. There are many varieties, such as those composed of claret, Madeira, &c.; but the ingredients of the real mint julep are as follows. I learned how to make them, and succeeded pretty well. Put into a tumbler about a dozen sprigs of the tender shoots of mint, upon them put a spoonful of white sugar, and equal proportions of peach and common brandy, so as to fill it up one-third, or perhaps a little less. Then take rasped or pounded ice, and fill up the tumbler. Epicures rub the lips of the tumbler with a piece of fresh pineapple, and the tumbler itself is very often incrusted outside with stalactites of ice. As the ice melts, you drink. I once overheard two ladies talking in the next room to me, and one of them said, 'Well, if I have a weakness for any one thing, it is for a mint julep!'—a very amiable weakness, and proving her good sense and good taste. They are, in fact, like the American ladies, irresistible."

88. Mint Julep.

(Use large bar glass.)
1 table-spoonful of white pulverized sugar.
2 1/2 do. water, mix well with a spoon.
Take three or four sprigs of fresh mint, and press them well in the sugar and water, until the flavor of the mint is extracted; add one and a half wine-glass of Cognac brandy, and fill the glass with fine shaved ice, then draw out the sprigs of mint and insert them in the ice with the stems downward, so that the leaves will be above, in the shape of a bouquet; arrange berries, and small pieces of sliced orange on top in a tasty manner, dash with Jamaica rum, and sprinkle white sugar on top. Place a straw as represented in the cut, and you have a julep that is fit for an emperor.

89. Brandy Julep.

(Use large bar glass)
The brandy julep is made with the same ingredients as the mint julep, omitting the fancy fixings.

90. Gin Julep.

(Use large bar glass.)
The gin julep is made with the same ingredients as the mint julep, omitting the fancy fixings.

91. Whiskey Julep.

(Use large bar glass.)

The whiskey julep is made the same as the mint julep, omitting all fruits and berries.

92. Pineapple Julep.

(For a party of five.) Peel, slice, and cut up a ripe pineapple into a glass bowl, add the juice of two oranges, a gill of raspberry syrup, a gill of maraschino, a gill of old gin, a bottle of sparkling Moselle, and about a pound of pure ice in shaves; mix, ornament with berries in season, and serve in flat glasses.

93. THE SMASH.

This beverage is simply a julep on a small plan.

94. Brandy Smash.

(Use small bar glass.)

1/2 table-spoonful of white sugar.

1 do. water.

1 wine-glass of brandy.

Fill two-thirds full of shaved ice, use two sprigs of mint, the same as in the recipe for mint julep. Lay two small pieces of orange on top, and ornament with berries in season.

95. Gin Smash.

(Use small bar glass.)

1/2 table-spoonful of white sugar.

1 do. water.

1 wine-glass of gin.

Fill two-thirds full of shaved ice, use two sprigs of mint, the same as in the recipe for mint julep. Lay two small pieces of orange on top, and ornament with berries in season.

96. Whiskey Smash.

(Use small bar glass.)

1/2 table-spoonful of white sugar.
1 do. water.
1 wine-glass of whiskey.
Fill two-thirds full of shaved ice, and use two sprigs of mint, the same as in the recipe for mint julep.

97. THE COBBLER.

Like the julep, this delicious potation is an American invention, although it is now a favorite in all warm climates. The "cobbler" does not require much skill in compounding, but to make it acceptable to the eye, as well as to the palate, it is necessary to display some taste in ornamenting the glass after the beverage is made. We give an illustration showing how a cobbler should look when made to suit an epicure.

98. Sherry Cobbler.

(Use large bar glass.)
2 wine-glasses of sherry.
1 table-spoonful of sugar.
2 or 3 slices of orange.
Fill a tumbler with shaved ice, shake well, and ornament with berries in season. Place a straw as represented in the wood-cut.

99. Champagne Cobbler. (One bottle of wine to four large bar glasses.) 1 table-spoonful of sugar. 1 piece each of orange and lemon peel. Fill the tumbler one-third full with shaved ice, and fill balance with wine, ornament in a tasty manner with berries in season. This beverage should be sipped through a straw.

100. Catawba Cobbler.

(Use large bar glass.)
1 teaspoonful of sugar dissolved in one table-spoonful of water.
2 wineglasses of wine.
Fill tumbler with shaved ice, and ornament with sliced orange and berries in season. Place a straw as described in the sherry cobbler.

101. Hock Cobbler.
(Use large bar glass.)

This drink is made the same way as the Catawba cobbler, using Hock wine instead of Catawba.

102. Claret Cobbler.
(Use large bar glass.)

This drink is made the same way as the Catawba cobbler, using claret wine instead of Catawba.

103. Sauterne Cobbler.
(Use large bar glass.)

The same as Catawba cobbler, using Sauterne instead of Catawba.

104. Whiskey Cobbler.
(Use large bar glass)

2 wine-glasses of whiskey.

1 tablespoonful of sugar.

2 or 3 slices of orange.

Fill tumbler with ice, and shake well. Imbibe through a straw.

105. THE COCKTAIL & CRUSTA.

The "Cocktail" is a modern invention, and is generally used on fishing and other sporting parties, although some patients insist that it is good in the morning as a tonic. The "Crusta" is an improvement on the " Cocktail," and is said to have been invented by Santina, a celebrated Spanish caterer.

106. Bottle Cocktail.
To make a splendid bottle of brandy cocktail, use the following ingredients:

2/3 brandy,

1/3 water.

1 pony-glass of Bogart's bitters.

1 wine-glass of gum syrup.

1/2 pony-glass of Curaçoa.

The author has always used this recipe in compounding the above beverage for connoisseurs. Whiskey and gin cocktails, in bottles, may be made by using the above recipe, and substituting those liquors instead of brandy.

107. Brandy Cocktail.

(Use small bar glass.)

3 or 4 dashes of gum syrup.

2 do. bitters (Bogart's).

1 wine-glass of brandy.

1 or 2 dashes of Curaçoa.

Squeeze lemon peel; fill one-third full of ice, and stir with a spoon.

108. Fancy Brandy Cocktail.

(Use small bar glass.)

This drink is made the same as the brandy cocktail, except that it is strained in a fancy wine-glass, and a piece of lemon peel thrown on top, and the edge of the glass moistened with lemon.

109. Whiskey Cocktail.

(Use small bar glass.)

3 or 4 dashes of gum syrup.

2 do. bitters (Bogart's).

1 wine-glass of whiskey, and a piece of lemon peel.

Fill one-third full of fine ice; shake and strain in a fancy red wine-glass.

110. Champagne Cocktail.

(One bottle of wine to every six large glasses.)

(Per glass.)

1/2 teaspoonful of sugar.

1 or 2 dashes of bitters.

Jerry Thomas
1 piece of lemon peel.
Fill tumbler one-third full of broken ice, and fill balance with wine. Shake well and serve.

111. Gin Cocktail.

(Use small bar glass.)

3 or 4 dashes of gum syrup.

2 do. bitters (Bogart's).

1 wine-glass of gin.

1 or 2 dashes of Curaçoa.

1 small piece lemon peel; fill one-third full of fine ice;
shake well, and strain in a glass.

112. Fancy Gin Cocktail.

(Use small bar glass.)

This drink is made the same as the gin cocktail, except that it is strained in a fancy wine-glass and a piece of lemon peel thrown on top, and the edge of the glass moistened with lemon.

113. Japanese Cocktail.

(Use small bar glass.)

1 table-spoonful of orgeat syrup.

1/2 teaspoonful of Bogart's bitters.

1 wine-glass of brandy.

1 or 2 pieces of lemon peel.

Fill the tumbler one-third with ice, and stir well with a spoon.

114. Jersey Cocktail.

(Use small bar glass.)

1 teaspoonful of sugar.

2 dashes of bitters.

Fill tumbler with cider, and mix well, with lemon peel on top.

115. Soda Cocktail.

(Use large bar glass.)

The same as Jersey cocktail, using soda-water instead of cider.

116. Brandy Crusta.

(Use small bar glass.)

Crusta is made the same as a fancy cocktail, with a little lemon juice and a small lump of ice added. First, mix the ingredients in a small tumbler, then take a fancy red wine-glass, rub a sliced lemon around the rim of the same, and dip it in pulverized white sugar, so that the sugar will adhere to the edge of the glass. Pare half a lemon the same as you would an apple (all in one piece) so that the paring will fit in the wine-glass, as shown in the cut, and strain the crusta from the tumbler into it. Then smile.

117. Whiskey Crusta.

(Use small bar glass.)

The whiskey crusta is made the same as the brandy crusta, using whiskey instead of brandy.

118. Gin Crusta.

(Use small bar glass.)

Gin crusta is made like the brandy crusta, using gin instead of brandy.

119. MULLS AND SANGAREES.

120. Mulled wine without Eggs.

To every pint of wine allow:

1 small tumblerful of water.

Sugar and spice to taste.

In making preparations like the above, it is very difficult to give the exact proportions of ingredients like sugar and spice, as what quantity might suit one person would be to another quite distasteful. Boil the spice in the water until the flavor is extracted, then add the wine and sugar, and bring the whole to the boiling point, then serve with strips of crisp, dry toast, or with biscuits. The spices usually used for mulled wine are cloves, grated nutmeg, and cinnamon or mace. Any kind of wine may be mulled, but port or claret are those usually selected for the purpose; and the latter requires a large proportion of sugar. The vessel that the wine is boiled in must be delicately clean.

121. Mulled Wine with Eggs.

1 quart of wine.

1 pint of water.

1 table-spoonful of allspice, and nutmeg to taste ; boil them together a few minutes; beat up six eggs with sugar to your taste; pour the boiling wine on the eggs, stirring it all the time. Be careful not to pour the eggs into the wine, or they will curdle.

122. Mulled Wine.

(With the whites of eggs.)

Dissolve 1 lb. sugar in two pints of hot water, to which add two and a half pints of good sherry wine, and let the mixture be set upon the fire until it is almost ready to boil. Meantime beat up the whites of twelve eggs to a froth, and pour into them the hot mixture, stirring rapidly. Add a little nutmeg.

123. Mulled Wine.

(In verse.)

"First, my dear madam, you must take
Nine eggs, which carefully you'll break—
Into a bowl you'll drop the white,
The yolks into another by it.
Let Betsy beat the whites with switch,
Till they appear quite frothed and rich—
Another hand the yolks must beat
With sugar, which will make them sweet;

How to Mix Drinks
Three or four spoonfuls may be'll do,
Though some, perhaps, would take but two.
Into a skillet next you'll pour
A bottle of good wine, or more—
Put half a pint of water, too,
Or it may prove too strong for you;
And while the eggs (by two) are beating,
The wine and water may be heating;
But, when it comes to boiling heat,
The yolks and whites together beat
With half a pint of water more—
Mixing them well, then gently pour
Into the skillet with the wine,
And stir it briskly all the time.
Then pour it off into a pitcher;
Grate nutmeg in to make it richer.
Then drink it hot, for he's a fool,
Who lets such precious liquor cool."

124. Mulled Claret.

(A la Lord Saltown.)
For this recipe see No. 191.

125. Port Wine Sangaree.

(Use small bar glass.)
1 1/2wine-glass of port wine.
1 teaspoonful of sugar.
Fill tumbler two-thirds with ice.
Shake well and grate nutmeg on top.

126. Sherry Sangaree.

(Use small bar glass.)
1 wine-glass of sherry.
1 teaspoonful of fine sugar.

Fill tumbler one-third with ice, and grate nutmeg on top.

127. Brandy Sangaree.

(Use small bar glass.)

The brandy sangaree is made with the same ingredients as the brandy toddy (see No. 133), omitting the nutmeg. Fill two-thirds full of ice, and dash about a teaspoonful of port wine, so that it will float on top.

128. Gin Sangaree.

(Use small bar glass.)

The gin sangaree is made with the same ingredients as the gin toddy (see No. 134), emitting the nutmeg. Fill two-thirds full of ice, and dash about a teaspoonful of port wine, so that it will float on tie top.

129. Ale Sangaree.

(Use large bar glass.)

1 teaspoonful of sugar, dissolved in a tablespoonful of water.
Fill the tumbler with ale, and grate nutmeg on top.

130. Porter Sangaree.

(Use large bar glass.)

This beverage is made the same as an ale sangaree, and is sometimes called porteree.

131. TODDIES AND SLINGS.

132. Apple Toddy.

(Use small bar glass.)
1 table-spoonful of fine white sugar.
1 wine-glass of cider brandy.
1/2 of a baked apple.

Fill the glass two-thirds full of boiling water, and grate a little nutmeg on top.

133. Brandy Toddy.

(Use small bar glass.)
1 teaspoonful of sugar.
1/2 wine-glass of water.
1 do. brandy.
1 small lump of ice.
Stir with a spoon.
For hot brandy toddy omit the ice, and use boiling water.

134. Whiskey Toddy.

(Use small bar glass.)
1 teaspoonful of sugar.
1/2 wine-glass of water.
1 do. whiskey.
1 small lump of ice.
Stir with a spoon.

135. Gin Toddy.

(Use small bar glass.)
1 teaspoonful of sugar.
1/2 wine-glass of water.
1 do. gin.
1 small lump of ice.
Stir with a spoon.

136. Brandy Sling.

(Use small bar glass.)
The brandy sling is made with the same ingredients as the brandy toddy, except you grate a little nutmeg on top.

137. Hot Whiskey Sling.

(Use small bar glass.)

1 wine-glass of whiskey.

Fill tumbler one-third full with boiling water, and grate nutmeg on top.

138. Gin Sling.

(Use small bar glass.)

The gin sling is made with the same ingredients as the gin toddy, except you grate a little nutmeg on top.

139. FIXES AND SOURS.

140. Brandy Fix.

(Use small bar glass.)

1 table-spoonful of sugar.

1/2 a wine-glass of water.

1/4 of a lemon.

1 do. brandy.

Fill a tumbler two-thirds full of shaved ice. Stir with a spoon, and dress the top with fruit in season.*

* The Santa Cruz fix is made by substituting Santa Cruz rum instead of brandy.

141, Gin Fix.

(Use small bar glass.)

1 table-spoonful of sugar.

1/2 a wine-glass of water. of a lemon.

1 do. gin.

Fill two-thirds full of shaved ice.

Stir with a spoon, and ornament the top with fruits in season.

142. Brandy Sour.

(Use small bar glass.)

The brandy sour is made with the same ingredients as the brandy fix, omitting all fruits except a small piece of lemon, the juice of which must be pressed in the glass.

143. Gin Sour.

(Use small bar glass.)

The gin sour is made with the same ingredients as the gin fix, omitting all fruits, except a small piece of lemon, . the juice of which must be pressed in the glass. †

† The Santa Cruz sour is made by substituting Santa Cruz rum instead of gin. In making fixes and sours be careful and put the lemon skin in the glass.

144. FLIP, NEGUS AND SHRUB.

145. Rum Flip.

—Which Dibdin has immortalized as the favorite beverage of sailors (although we believe they seldom indulge in it) —is made by adding a gill of rum to the beer, or substituting rum and water, when malt liquor cannot be procured. The essential in "flips" of all sorts is, to produce the smoothness by repeated pouring back and forward between two vessels, and beating up the eggs well in the first instance; the sweetening and spices according to taste.

146. Rum Flip.

(Another method.)

Keep grated ginger and nutmeg with a little fine dried lemon peel, rubbed together in a mortar.

To make a quart of flip:—Put the ale on the fire to warm, and beat up three or four eggs with four ounces of moist sugar, a teaspoonful of grated nutmeg or ginger, and a gill of good old rum or brandy. When the ale is near to boil, put it into one pitcher, and the rum and eggs, &c., into another; turn it from one pitcher to another till it is as smooth as cream.

147. Ale Flip.

Put on the fire in a saucepan one quart of ale, and let it boil; have ready the whites of two eggs and the yolks of four, well beaten up separately; add them by degrees to four table-spoonfuls of moist sugar, and half a nutmeg grated. When all are well mixed, pour on the boiling ale by degrees, beating up the mixture continually; then pour it rapidly backward and forward from one jug to another, keeping one jug raised high above the other, till the flip is. smooth and finely frothed. This is a good remedy to take at the commencement of a cold.

148. Egg Flip.

Put a quart of ale in a tinned saucepan on the fire to boil; in the mean time, beat up the yolks of four, with the whites of two eggs, adding four table.spoonfuls of brown sugar and a little nutmeg; pour on the ale by degrees, beating up, so as to prevent the mixture from curdling; then pour back and forward repeatedly from vessel to vessel, raising the hand to as great a height as possible— which process produces the smoothness and frothing essential to the good quality of the flip. This is excellent for a cold, and, from its fleecy appearance, is sometimes designated " a yard of flannel."

149. Egg Flip.

(Another method.)

Beat up, in a jug, four new-laid eggs, omitting two of the whites; add half a dozen large lumps of sugar, and rub these well in the eggs, pour in boiling water, about half a pint at a time, and when the jug is nearly full, throw in two tumblers of Cognac brandy, and one of old Jamaica rum.

150. Brandy Flip.

(Use small bar glass.)

1 teaspoonful of sugar.

1 wine-glass of brandy.
Fill the tumbler one-third full of hot water, mix, and place a toasted
cracker on top, and grate nutmeg over it.

151. Port Wine Negus.

To every pint of port wine allow:
1 quart of boiling water.
1/4 lb. of loaf-sugar.
1 lemon.
Grated nutmeg to taste.
Put the wine into a jug, rub some lumps of sugar (equal 1/4 to lb.) on the
lemon rind until all the yellow part of the skin is absorbed, then squeeze
the juice and strain it. Add the sugar and lemon-juice to the port wine, with
the grated nutmeg; pour over it the boiling water, cover the jug, and when
the beverage has cooled a little, it will be fit for use. Negus may also be
made of sherry, or any other sweet wine, but it is more usually made of
port. This beverage derives its name from Colonel Negus, who is said to
have invented it.

152. Port Wine Negus.

(Use small bar glass.)
1 wine-glass of port wine.
1 teaspoonful of sugar. Fill tumbler one-third full with hot water.

153. Soda Negus. A most refreshing and elegant beverage, particularly for
those who do not take punch or grog after supper, is thus made:
Put half a pint of port wine, with four lumps of sugar, three cloves, and
enough grated nutmeg to cover a shilling, into a saucepan; warm it well,
but do not suffer it to boil; pour it into a bowl or jug, and upon the warm
wine decant a bottle of soda-water. You will have an effervescing and
delicious negus by this means.

154. Cherry Shrub.

Pick ripe acid cherries from the stem, put them in an earthen pot; place that in an iron pot of water; boil till the juice is extracted; strain it through a cloth thick enough to retain the pulp, and sweeten it to your taste. When perfectly clear, bottle it, sealing the cork. By first putting a gill of brandy into each bottle, it will keep through the summer. It is delicious mixed with water. Irish or Monongahela whiskey will answer instead of the brandy, though not as good.

155. White Currant Shrub.

Strip the fruit, and prepare in a jar, as for jelly; strain the juice, of which put two quarts to one gallon of rum, and two pounds of lump-sugar; strain through a jelly-bag.

156. Currant Shrub.

1 lb. of sugar.
1 pint of strained currant juice.
Boil it gently eight or ten minutes, skimming it well; take it off, and when lukewarm, add half a gill of brandy to every pint of shrub. Bottle tight.

157. Raspberry Shrub.

1 quart of vinegar.
3 quarts of ripe raspberries.
After standing a day, strain it, adding to each pint a pound of sugar, and skim it clear, while boiling about half an hour. Put a wine-glass of brandy to each pint of the shrub, when cool. Two spoonfuls of this mixed with a tumbler of water, is an excellent drink in warm weather, and in fevers.

158. Brandy Shrub.

To the thin rinds of two lemons, and the juice of five, add two quarts of brandy; cover it for three days, then add a quart of sherry and two pounds of loaf-sugar, run it through a jelly-bag, and bottle it.

159, Rum Shrub.

Put three pints of orange juice, and one pound of loaf sugar to a gallon of rum. Put all into a cask, and leave it for six weeks, when it will be ready for use.

160. English Rum Shrub.

To three gallons of best Jamaica rum, add a quart of orange juice, a pint of lemon juice, with the peels of the latter fruit cut very thin, and six pounds of powdered white sugar. Let these be covered close, and remain so all night; next day boil three pints of fresh milk, and let it get cold, then pour it on the spirit and juice, mix them Well, and let it stand for an hour. Filter it through a flannel bag lined with blotting-paper, into bottles; cork down as soon as each is filled.

161. FANCY DRINKS.

The following miscellaneous collection of fancy beverages, embraces a number of French, Spanish, English, Russian, Italian, German, and American recipes.

162. Santina's Pousse Cafe.

(Use small wine-glass.)

This delicious drink is from a recipe by SANTINA, proprietor of "Santina's Saloon" a celebrated Spanish Café, in New Orleans.

1/3 brandy (cognac).

1/3 maraschino.

1/3 Curaçoa.

Mix well.

163. Parisian Pousse Cafe.

(Use small wine-glass.)

2/5 Curaçoa.

2/5Kirschwasser.

1/5 Chartreuse.

Jerry Thomas
This is a celebrated Parisian drink.

164. Faivre's Pousse Cafe.

(Use small wine-glass.)
1/3 Parisian pousse café (as above).
1/3 Kirschwasser.
1/3 Curaçoa.
This celebrated drink is from the recipe of M. FAIVRE, a popular
proprietor of a "French Saloon" in New York.

165. Pousse l'Amour.

This delightful French drink is described in the above engraving. To mix it
fill a small wine-glass half full of maraschino, then put in the pure yolk of
an egg, surround the yolk with vanilla cordial, and dash the top with
Cognac brandy.

166. Brandy Champerelle.

(Use small wine-glass.)
1/3 brandy.
1/3 Bogart's bitters.
1/3 Curaçoa.
This is a delicious French cafe drink.

167. Brandy Scaffa.

(Use wino-glass.)
1/2 brandy.
1/2 maraschino.
2 dashes of bitters.

168. Sleeper.

To a gill of old rum add one ounce of sugar, two yolks of eggs, and the
juice of half a lemon; boil half a pint of water with six cloves, six

coriander-seeds, and a bit of cinnamon; whisk all together, and strain them into a tumbler.

169. Claret and Champagne Cup, à la Brunow.

(For a party of twenty.)

The following claret and champagne cup ought, from its excellence, to be called the nectar of the Czar, as it is so highly appreciated in Russia, where for many years it has enjoyed a high reputation amongst the aristocracy of the Muscovite empire. Proportions:

3 bottles of claret.

2/3 pint of Curaçoa.

1 do. sherry.

1/2 do. brandy.

2 wine-glasses* ratafia of raspberries.

3 oranges and 1 lemon, cut in slices.

Some sprigs of green balm, and of borage, a small piece of rind of cucumber.

2 bottles of German Seltzer-water.

3 do. soda-water.

Stir this together, and sweeten with capillaire or pounded sugar, until it ferments; let it stand one hour, strain it, and ice it well; it is then fit for use. Serve in small glasses.

The same for champagne cup: champagne instead of claret; noyau instead of ratafia.

This quantity is for an evening party of twenty persons. For a smaller number reduce the proportions.

* 170. Ratafias.

Every liqueur made by infusions is called ratifia; that is, when the spirit is made to imbibe thoroughly the aromatic flavor and color of the fruit steeped in it: when this has taken place, the liqueur is drawn off, and sugar added to it; it is then filtered and bottled. See recipe No. 306 in " The Manual for the Manufacture of Cordials, etc.," in the latter part of this work.

171. Balaklava Nectar. (By Soyer.)
(For a party of fifteen.)

Thinly peel the rind of half a lemon, shred it fine, and put it in a punch-bowl; add two table-spoonfuls of crushed sugar, and the juice of two lemons, the half of a small cucumber sliced thin, with the peel on; toss it up several times, then add 2 bottles of soda-water, 2 of claret, 1 of champagne, stir well together, and serve.

172. Crimean Cup, a la Marmora.
(From a recipe by the celebrated Soyer.)

(For a party of thirty.)

1 quart of syrup of orgeat.

1 pint of Cognac brandy.

1/2 do. maraschino.

1/2 do. Jamaica rum.

2 bottles of champagne.

2 do. soda-water.

6 ounces of sugar.

4 middling-sized lemons.

Thinly peel the lemons, and place the rind in a bowl with the sugar, macerate them well for a minute or two, in order to extract the flavor from the lemon. Next squeeze the juice of the lemons upon this, add two bottles of soda-water, and stir well till the sugar is dissolved; pour in the syrup of orgeat, and whip the mixture well with an egg-whisk, in order to whiten the composition. Then add the brandy, rum and maraschino, strain the whole into the punch-bowl, and just before serving add the champagne, which should be well iced. While adding the champagne, stir well with the ladle; this will render the cup creamy and mellow.

Half the quantity given here, or even less, may be made; this recipe being for a party of thirty.

173. Crimean Cup, a la Wyndham.
(For a party of five.)

Thinly peel the rind of half an orange, put it into a bowl, with a table-spoonful of crushed sugar, and macerate with the ladle for a minute; then add one large wine-glass of maraschino, half one of Cognac, half one of Curaçoa. Mix well together, pour in two bottles of soda-water, and one of champagne, during which time work it up and down with the punch-ladle, and it is ready.

Half a pound of pure ice is a great improvement.

174. Tom and Jerry.

(Use punch-bowl for the mixture.)
5 lbs. sugar.
12 eggs.
1/2 small glass of Jamaica rum.
1 1/2 teaspoonful of ground cinnamon,
1/2 do. do. cloves,
1/2 do. do allspice.

Beat the whites of the eggs to a stiff froth, and the yolks until they are as thin as water, then mix together and add the spice and rum, thicken with sugar until the mixture attains the consistence of a light batter.

To deal out Tom and Jerry to customers: . Take a small bar glass, and to one table-spoonful of tho above mixture, add one wine-glass of brandy, and fill the glass with boiling water, grate a little nutmeg on top.

Adepts at the bar, in serving Tom and Jerry, sometimes adopt a mixture of £ brandy, i Jamaica rum, and J Santa Cruz rum, instead of brandy plain. This compound is usually mixed and kept in a bottle, and a wine-glassful is used to each tumbler of Tom and Jerry.

N. B.—A tea-spoonful of cream of tartar, or about as much carbonate of soda as you can get on a dime, will prevent the sugar from settling to the bottom of the mixture. This drink is sometimes called Copenhagen, and sometimes Jerry Thomas.

175. White Tiger's Milk.

(From recipe in the possession of Thomas Dunn English, Esq.)
1/2 gill apple-jack.
1/2 do. peach brandy.
1/2 teaspoonful of aromatic tincture.*
Sweeten with white sugar to taste.

The white of an egg beaten to a stiff foam.

1 quart of pure milk.

Pour in the mixed liquors to the milk, stirring all the white till all is well mixed, then sprinkle with nutmeg. The above recipe is sufficient to make a full quart of "white tiger's milk;" if more is wanted, you can increase the above proportions. If you want to prepare this beverage for a party of twenty, use one gallon of milk to one pint of apple-jack, &c.

* Aromatic Tincture.—Take of ginger, cinnamon, orange peel, each one ounce; valerian half an ounce, alcohol two quarts, macerate in a close vessel for fourteen days, then filter through unsized paper. Mix well, ornament with berries in season, and cool with shaved ice.

176. White Lion.

(Use small bar glass.)

1 1/2 teaspoonful of pulverized white sugar.

1/2 a lime (squeeze out juice and put rind in glass).

1 wine-glass Santa Cruz rum.

1/2 teaspoonful of Curaçoa.

1/2 do. raspberry syrup.

177. Locomotive.

Put two yolks of eggs into a goblet with an ounce of honey, a little essence of cloves, and a liqueur-glass of Curaçoa; add a pint of high Burgundy made hot, whisk well together, and serve hot in glasses.

178. Bishop.

(A la Prusse.)

A favorite beverage, made with claret or port. It is prepared as follows: roast four good-sized bitter oranges till they are of a pale-brown color, lay them in a tureen, and put over them half a pound of pounded loaf-sugar, and three glasses of claret; place the cover on the tureen and let it stand till the next day. When required for use, put the tureen into a pan of boiling water, press the oranges with a spoon, and run the juice through a sieve; then boil the remainder of the bottle of claret, taking care that it does not burn; add it to the strained juice, and serve it warm in glasses. Port wine will answer the purpose as well as claret. "Bishop" is sometimes made with the above materials, substituting lemons instead of oranges, but this is not often done when claret is used. See recipe No 38, in "The Manual for the Manufacture of Cordials, etc." at the latter part of this work.

179. Bishop.
(Another recipe.)

Stick an orange full of cloves, and roast it before a fire. When brown enough, cut it in quarters, and pour over it a quart of hot port wine, add sugar to the taste, let the mixture simmer for half an hour.

180. Archbishop.

The same as Bishop, substituting claret for the port.

181. Cardinal.

Same as above, substituting champagne for claret.

182. Pope.

Same as above, substituting Burgundy for champagne.

183. A Bishop.
(Protestant)

4 table-spoons of white sugar.

2 tumblers of water.

1 lemon, in slices.

1 bottle of claret.

4 table-spoons of Santa Cruz or Jamaica. Ice.

184. Knickerbocker.
(Use small bar glass.)

1/2 a lime, or lemon, squeeze out the juice, and put rind and juice in the glass.

Jerry Thomas

2 teaspoonfuls of raspberry syrup.

1 wine-glass Santa Cruz rum.

1/2 teaspoonful of Curaçoa.

Cool with shaved ice; shake up well, and ornament with berries in season. If this is not sweet enough, put in a little more raspberry syrup.

185. Rumfustian.

This is the singular name bestowed upon a drink very much in vogue with English sportsmen, after their return from a day's shooting, and is concocted thus:

The yolks of a dozen eggs are well whisked up, and put into a quart of strong beer; to this is added a pint of gin; a bottle of sherry is put into a saucepan, with a stick of cinnamon, a nutmeg grated, a dozen large lumps of sugar, and the rind of a lemon peeled very thin; when the wine boils, it is poured upon the gin and beer, and the whole drunk hot.

186. Claret Cup.

To a bottle of thin claret add half a pint of cold water, a table-spoonful of finely powdered sugar, and a teaspoonful of cinnamon, cloves, and allspice, finely powdered and mixed together. Mix all well together, then add half the thin rind of a small lemon. This is a delicious summer beverage for evening parties. See No. 191.

187. Porter Cup.

Mix in a tankard or covered jug a bottle of porter, and an equal quantity of table-ale; pour in a glass of brandy, a dessert-spoonful of syrup of ginger, add three or four lumps of sugar, and half a nutmeg grated; cover it down, and expose it to the cold for half an hour; just before sending it to table, stir in a teaspoonful of carbonate of soda. Add the fresh-cut rind of a cucumber.

188. English Curaçoa.

Cut away the peel of oranges very thin, until you have obtained half a dozen ounces of it; put these into a quart bottle, and then pour in a pint of genuine whiskey. Cork the bottle down tightly, and let the rind remain infused for ten or twelve days, giving the bottle a good shake as often as you have an opportunity for so doing; at the end of this period, take out the orange peel, and fill the bottle with clarified syrup, shake it well with the spirit, and let it remain for three days. Pour a teacupful of the liqueur into a mortar, and beat up a drachm of powdered alum, and an equal quantity of carbonate of potash; pour this, when well mixed, into the bottle, shake it well, and in a week you will find the Curaçoa perfectly transparent, and equal in flavor to that imported from Malines, or any other place in the universe.

189. Italian Lemonade.

Pare and press two dozen lemons; pour the juice on the peels, and let it remain on them all night; in the morning add two pounds of loaf-sugar, a quart of good sherry, and three quarts of boiling water. Mix well, add a quart of boiling milk, and strain it through a jelly-bag till clear.

190. Quince Liqueur.

2 quarts of quince juice.

4 do. Cognac brandy.

2 1/2 lbs. of white sugar.

12 ounces of bitter almonds, bruised.

1 lb. of coriander-seeds.

36 cloves.

Grate a sufficient number of quinces to make 2 quarts of juice, and squeeze them through a jelly-bag. Mix the ingredients all together, and put them in a demijohn, and shake them well every day for ten days. Then strain the liquid through a jelly-bag till it is perfectly clear, and bottle for use. This is a delightful liqueur, and can be relied upon, as it is from a recipe in the possession of a lady who is famous for concocting delicious potations.

191. Claret Cup, or Mulled Claret.

(A la Lord Saltoun.)

Jerry Thomas

Peel one lemon fine, add to it some white pounded sugar; pour over one glass of sherry, then add a bottle of claret (vin ordinaire, the best), and sugar to taste; add a sprig of verbena, one bottle of soda-water, and nutmeg, if you like it. For cup, strain and ice it well. For mull, heat it and serve it hot.

192. Bottled Velvet.

(A la Sir John Bayley.)

A bottle of Moselle, half a pint of sherry, the peel of a lemon, not too much, so as to have the flavor predominate; two table-spoonfuls of sugar; add a sprig of verbena; all must be well mixed, and then strained and iced.

193. Champagne, Hock or Chablis Cup.

(A la Goodriche.)

Dissolve four or five lumps of sugar in a quarter of a pint of boiling water, with a little very thin lemon peel; let it stand a quarter of an hour; add one bottle of the above wines, and a sprig of verbena, a small glass of sherry; half a pint of water. Mix well, and let stand half an hour; strain, and ice it well.

194. Cider Nectar.

(A la Harold Littledale.)

1 quart of cider.

1 bottle of soda-water.

1 glass of sherry.

1 small glass of brandy.

Juice of half a lemon, peel of quarter of a lemon; sugar and nutmeg to taste; a sprig of verbena. Flavor it to taste with extract of pineapple. Strain, and ice it all well. This is a delicious beverage, and only requires to be tasted to be appreciated.

195. Badminton.

Peel half of a middle-sized cucumber, and put it into a silver cup, with four ounces of powdered sugar a little nutmeg, and a bottle of claret. When the

sugar is thoroughly dissolved, pour in a bottle of soda-water, and it is fit
for use.

196. MISCELLANEOUS DRINKS.

197. Blue Blazer.

(Use two large silver-plated mugs, with handles.)

1 wine-glass of Scotch whiskey.

1 do. boiling water.

Put the whiskey and the boiling water in one mug, ignite the liquid with
fire, and while blazing mix both ingredients by pouring them four or five
times from one mug to the other, as represented in the cut. If well done this
will have the appearance of a continued stream of liquid fire.

Sweeten with one teaspoonful of pulverized white sugar, and serve in a
small bar tumbler, with a piece of lemon peel.

The "blue blazer" does not have a very euphonious or classic name, but it
tastes better to the palate than it sounds to the ear. A beholder gazing for
the first time upon an experienced artist, compounding this beverage,
would naturally come to the conclusion that it was a nectar for Pluto rather
than Bacchus. The novice in mixing this beverage should be careful not to
scald himself. To become proficient in throwing the liquid from one mug
to the other, it will be necessary to practise for some time with cold water.

198. "Jerry Thomas'" own Decanter Bitters.

1/4 lb. of raisins.

2 ounces of cinnamon.

1 do. snake-root.

1 lemon and 1 orange cut in slices.

1 ounce of cloves.

1 do. allspice.

Fill decanter with Santa Cruz rum.

Bottle and serve out in pony glasses. As fast as the bitters is used fill up
again with rum.

199. Burnt Brandy and Peach.

(Use small bar glass.)

This drink is very popular in the Southern States, where it is sometimes used as a cure for diarrhoea.

1 wine-glass of Cognac	Burnt in a
1/2 table-spoon of white sugar	Aaucer or plate

2 or 3 slices of dried peaches

Place the dried fruit in a glass and pour the liquid over them.

200. Black Stripe.

(Use small bar glass.)
1 wine-glass of Santa Cruz rum.
1 table-spoonful of molasses.

This drink can either be made in summer or winter: if in the former season, mix in 1 table-spoonful of water, and cool with shaved ice; if in the latter, fill up the tumbler with boiling water. Grate a little nutmeg on top.

201. Peach and Honey.

(Use small bar glass)
1 table-spoonful of honey.
1 wine-glass of peach brandy.
Stir with a spoon.

202. Grin and Pine.

(Use wine-glass.)

Split a piece of the heart of a green pine log into fine splints, about the size of a cedar lead-pencil, take 2 ounces of the same and put into a quart decanter, and fill the decanter with gin.

Let the pine soak for two hours, and the gin will be ready to serve.

203. Gin and Tansy.

(Use wine-glass.)

Fill a quart decanter 1/3 full of tansy, and pour in gin to fill up the balance 1/3 tansy to 2/3 gin. Serve to customers in a wine-glass.

204. Gin and "Wormwood.

(Use small bar glass.)

Put three or four sprigs of wormwood into a quart decanter, and fill up with gin.

The above three drinks are not much used except in small country villages.

205. Scotch Whiskey Skin.

(Use small bar glass)

1 wine-glass of Scotch whiskey.

1 piece of lemon peel.

Fill the tumbler one-half full with boiling water.

206. Columbia Skin.

(Use small bar glass.)

This is a Boston drink, and is made the same as a whiskey skin.

207. Hot Spiced Rum.

(Use Email bar glass.)

1 teaspoonful of sugar.

1 wine-glass of Jamaica rum.

1 teaspoonful of mixed spices, (allspice and cloves.)

1 piece of butter as large as half of a chestnut.

Fill tumbler with hot water.

208. Hot Rum.

(Use small bar glass.)

This drink is made the same as the hot spiced rum, omitting the spices, and grating a little nutmeg on top.

209. Stone Fence.

(Use large bar glass.)
1 wine-glass of whiskey (Bourbon).
2 or 3 small lumps of ice.
Fill up the glass with sweet cider.

210. Absinthe.

(Use small bar glass.)
1 wine-glass of absinthe.
Pour water, drop by drop, until the glass is full. Never use a spoon.

211. Rhine "Wine and Seltzer-Water.

(Use large bar glass.)
Fill large bar glass half full with Rhine wine, and fill balance with Seltzer-water. This is a German drink, and is not very likely to be called for at an American bar.

212. "Arf and Art"

(Use large bar glass.)
In London this drink is made by mixing half porter and half ale, in America it is made by mixing half new and half old ale.

213. Brandy Straight.

(Use small bar glass)

In serving this drink you simply put a piece of ice in a tumbler, and hand to your customer, with the bottle of brandy. This is very safe for a steady drink, but though a straight beverage, it is often used on a bender.

214. Gin Straight.

(Use small bar glass)

Same as brandy straight, substituting gin for brandy.

215. Pony Brandy.

(Use pony-glass.)

Fill the pony-glass with (Sasarac) best brandy, and hand it to your customer.

216. Brandy and Soda.

(Sometimes called Stone Wall.)

(Use large bar glass.)

1 wine-glass of Cognac brandy.

1/3 glass of fine ice.

Fill up with plain soda.

217. Brandy and Gum.

(Use small bar glass.)

Same as brandy straight, with one dash of gum syrup.

218. Sherry and Egg.

(Use small bar glass.)

1 Egg.

1 wine-glass of sherry.

219. Sherry and Bitters.

1 dash of bitters.

1 wine-glass of sherry.

220. Sherry and Ice.

(Use small bar glass.)

Jerry Thomas
Put two lumps of ice in a glass, and fill with wine.

221. TEMPERANCE DRINKS.

222. Lemonade*

(Use large bar glass.)

The juice of half a lemon.

1 1/2 table-spoonful of sugar.

2 or three pieces of orange.

1 table-spoonful of raspberry or strawberry syrup.

Fill the tumbler one-half full with shaved ice, the balance with water; dash with port wine, and ornament with fruits in season.

* See recipes Nos. 255, 256, and 257 in "The Manual for the Manufacture of Cordials, etc.," at the latter part of this work.

223. Plain Lemonade.

(From a recipe by the celebrated Soyer.)

Cut in very thin slices 3 lemons, put them in a basin, add half a pound of sugar, either white or brown; bruise all together, add a gallon of water, and stir well. It is then ready.

224. Lemonade.

(Fine for parties.)

The rind of 2 lemons

juice of 3 large

1/2 do. lb. of loaf-sugar.

1 quart of boiling water.

Rub some of the sugar, in lumps, on two of the lemons until they have imbibed all the oil from them, and put it with the remainder of the sugar into a jug; add the lemon juice (but no pips), and pour over the whole a quart of boiling water. When the sugar is dissolved, strain the lemonade through a piece of muslin, and, when cool, it will be ready for use.

The lemonade will be much improved by having the white of an egg beaten up with it; a little sherry mixed with it also makes this beverage much nicer.

225. Orangeade.

This agreeable beverage is made the same way as lemonade, substituting oranges for lemons.

226. Orgeat Lemonade.

(Use large bar glass.)
1/2 wine-glass of orgeat syrup.
The juice of half of a lemon.
Fill the tumbler one-third full of ice, and balance with water. Shake well, and ornament with berries in season.

227. Ginger Lemonade.

Boil twelve pounds and a half of lump-sugar for twenty minutes in ten gallons of water; clear it with the whites of six eggs. Bruise half a pound of common ginger, boil with the liquor, and then pour it upon ten lemons pared. When quite cold, put it in a cask, with two table-spoonfuls of yeast, the lemons sliced, and half an ounce of isinglass. Bung up the cask the next day; it will be ready in two weeks.

228. Soda Nectar.

(Use large tumbler.)
Juice of 1 lemon.
3/4 tumblerful of water.
Powdered white sugar to taste.
1/2 small teaspoonful of carbonate of soda.
Strain the juice of the lemon, and add it to the water, with sufficient white sugar to sweeten the whole nicely. When well mixed, put in the soda, stir well, and drink while the mixture is in an effervescing state.

229. Drink for the Dog Days.

A bottle of soda-water poured into a large goblet, in which a lemon ice has been placed, forms a deliciously cool and refreshing drink; but should be taken with some care, and positively avoided whilst you are very hot.

230. Sherbet.

Eight ounces of carbonate of soda, six ounces of tartaric acid, two pounds of loaf-sugar (finely powdered), three drachms of essence of lemon. Let the powders be very dry. Mix them intimately, and keep them for use in a wide-mouthed bottle, closely corked. Put two good-sized teaspoonfuls into a tumbler; pour in half a pint of cold water, stir briskly, and drink off.

231. Lemonade Powders.

One pound of finely-powdered loaf-sugar, one ounce of tartaric or citric acid, and twenty drops of essence of lemon. Mix, and keep very dry. Two or three teaspoonfuls of this stirred briskly in a tumbler of water will make a very pleasant glass of lemonade. If effervescent lemonade be desired, one ounce of carbonate of soda must be added to the above.

232. Draught Lemonade, or Lemon Sherbet.

Four lemons sliced, four ounces of lump-sugar, one quart of boiling water. Very fine. A cheaper drink may be made thus:—One ounce of cream of tartar, one ounce of tartaric or citric acid, the juice and peel of two lemons, and half a pound, or more, of loaf-sugar. The sweetening must be regulated according to taste.

233. Imperial Drink for Families.

Two ounces of cream of tartar, the juice and peel of two or three lemons, and half a pound of coarse sugar. Put these into a gallon pitcher, and pour on boiling water. When cool, it will be fit for use.

234. Nectar.

One drachm of citric acid, one scruple of bicarbonate of potash, one ounce of white sugar, powdered. Fill a soda water bottle nearly full of water, drop in the potash and sugar, and lastly the citric acid. Cork the bottle up immediately, and shake. As soon as the crystals are dissolved, the nectar is fit for use. It may be colored with a small portion of cochineal.

235. Raspberry, strawberry, currant, or Orange Effervescing Draughts.

Take one quart of the juice of either of the above fruits, filter it, and boil it into a syrup, with one pound of powdered loaf-sugar. To this add one ounce and a half of tartaric acid. When cold put it into a bottle, and keep it well corked. When required for use, fill a half-pint turn bier three parts full of water, and add two table-spoonfuls of the syrup. Then stir in briskly a small teaspoonful of carbonate of soda, and a very delicious drink will be formed. The color may be improved by adding a very small portion of cochineal to the syrup at the time of boiling.

236. Ginger Wine.

Put twelve pounds of loaf-sugar and six ounces of powdered ginger into six gallons of water; let it boil for an hour, then beat up the whites of half a dozen eggs with a whisk, and mix them well with the liquor. When quite cold put it into a barrel, with six lemons cut into slices, and a cupful of yeast; let it work for three days, then put in the bung. In a week's time you may bottle it, and it will be ready for immediate use.

MANUAL FOR THE MANUFACTURE OF CORDIALS,
LIQUORS, FANCY SYRUPS, &C. &C.
AFTER THE MOST COMMON AND APPROVED METHODS NOW
USED IN THE DISTILLATION OF LIQUORS AND BEVERAGES,
DESIGNED FOR THE SPECIAL USE OF MANUFACTURERS,
DEALERS IN WINES AND SPIRITS, GROCERS, TAVERN KEEPERS
AND PRIVATE FAMILIES. THE SAME BEING ADAPTED TO THE
TRADE OF THE UNITED STATES AND THE CANADAS. BY PROF.
CHRISTIAN SCHULTZ, PRACTICAL CHEMIST AND DISTILLER.

INTRODUCTION. TO THE READER.

THE Author of the following work, in presenting it as a useful and valuable practical Manual to Manufacturers, Distillers, and Dealers in Cordials, Liquors, etc., in this country, thinks, that long experience as a practical distiller and vender of the above articles, gives him strong claims to the favorable considerations of the public at large.

A close and uniform practice of fifteen years in Switzerland, as well as in the city of New York; a thorough acquaintance with the method used in the best distilleries in Paris and Bordeaux; and manufacturing, as he has been, for many years for wholesale houses in this city, he flatters himself that in this Manual he has furnished all the facilities necessary, the recipes used, and the directions required, for the best preparations of the most celebrated Cordials, Liquors, Syrups, etc., ever yet introduced. The book contains the easiest, shortest, and the most economical manner of preparing the various articles; the style is concise and clear, so that it can be readily comprehended, and its matter, with great method and order, is alphabetically arranged under proper heads and references. Measures and weights referred to are those of the United States.

The Author, in this compendium, did not deem it necessary to describe the raw materials generally used in macerating and distilling. Such a description would only unnecessarily enlarge the work, thereby increasing the price, with but little or no advantage to the reader. A well informed and practical druggist will at once be able to understand, and properly furnish, the articles contained in each recipe.

The first to be.described are the "Manufacturing Instruments" for without these nothing can be effected. The arrangements and preparations of the articles described in this work, do not contemplate an expensive and costly apparatus, nevertheless the author recommends that the best materials and most substantial instruments should be provided, by reason of their durability, and the certainty of obtaining in its perfection a good product.

The instruments deemed indispensable in the process of distilling are as follows:—first, a furnace; second, two boilers of tinned copper; third, a copper skimmer; fourth, a few filter-bags, filtering-holders, and a percolator; fifth, tubs and pails for various uses; sixth, measures from one gallon to that of the smallest; seventh, weights and scales; eighth, areometer; ninth, funnels; tenth, alcohol lamps, with tinned dishes for different colors of bottle wax; eleventh, a cork-press and syphon; twelfth, casks, demijohns, bottles.

Those who wish to engage in this business on a large scale, would do well to purchase a brass mortar; one of iron would often change the color of the material; one of stone is required for the preparation of syrup of orgeat. Sieves must also be provided for separating the coarse powdered materials from the fine, and a large knife for cutting and preparing roots, etc., etc., for the powdered state.

Necessary Preparations.—There should always be on hand, well clarified white and brown sugar syrups, put up in well-corked demijohns and labelled. Clean spirit, or rectified whiskey, alcohol of 95 per cent.; sugar coloring for brandies, rum, etc.; tincture of turmeric, for essence of peppermint; tincture of cochineal for red cordials. All other colors prepared when wanted. Flavoring essences can be prepared in some larger quantity when wanted, and put up in bottles, labelled for further use.

Fruit syrups, such as raspberry, strawberry, etc., are prepared in summer; others, such as orgeat, gum, sarsaparilla, etc., at any season.

In preparing the following work, the author has had in view brevity and utility. He believes that such a Manual is much wanted in the business of distillation, and has spared no pains, which thorough experience and a practical knowledge of the subject could bring to his aid. It contains four hundred improved recipes of the various preparations now known, and each one can be readily referred to from the excellent alphabetical arrangements adopted.

To the liberal patronage and favorable consideration of his friends and the public at large, he most respectfully submits the result of his labors.

NEW YORK, January 2, 1862.

DESCRIPTION OF THE APPARATUS USED FOR MANUFACTURING LIQUORS, CORDIALS, SYRUPS, &c., &c.,

Together with some ideas on Distillation, Filtration and Clarification. THE first and most important is the furnace: temporary accommodations, under the name of furnaces, only prolong the operations of the distiller, and render his products very often imperfect. With a good fire, and proper apparatus, work can be accomplished with readiness and comparative ease; whereas, the ordinary measures of every day's experiments often fail of success.

The portable furnace (1) is most excellent for boilers of from 5 to 10 gallons, and may be used as a heating or cooking stove for families, as well as for the purposes of distillation. Coal can be filled in without moving the boiler, it having a good draught of air, and being laid out with firebricks, with a fall-grate for extinguishing the coal after using. The above can be obtained, ready-made, of J. Murphy, at No. 256 Water street, complete for $5.

The concurbit, or boiler (2), belonging to the furnace, contains 10 gallons of liquid, and is formed of tinned copper—the smaller part of the bottom standing on the firebricks, while the upper bottom covers the top of the furnace. This construction enables the first heat of the coal to give its whole strength on the under bottom, and rising up by the door, continues around the boiler, between the top and the brick-work, and in the stove-pipe. By this process, time and coal are both saved.

2. Distillation

Consists essentially in converting a liquid into vapor in a close vessel, by means of heat, and then conveying the vapor into another cool vessel, where it is condensed again into a liquid.

To accomplish this, the liquids are placed in the boiler (2), and when heat is applied to the boiler, spirit begins to rise in vapor at 176° (degrees), and water is converted into vapor at 212° (degrees). These vapors pass from the boiler through the tube into the worm (3), and in passing through the worm, become condensed by the cold. The refrigerator, or worm-tub (4), must be kept full, by a constant stream of cold water, or else the water at the bottom will be cold, while that of the surface will be very hot. The cold water is supplied at 5, and escapes at 6.

With respect to the practical part of distilling, we shall observe that the heat should, in all cases, be as gentle and uniform as possible. Accidents may be effectually prevented by distilling spirits in a water bath, which, if sufficiently large, will perform the operation with all the dispatch requisite for the most extensive business. The vessel in which the distillation is effected ought to be immersed in another filled with water up to the neck. The process will thus be managed as expeditiously as if the vessel were placed over an open fire, and without the apprehension of being disappointed by having your spirits burned; nor will it be necessary at any time to raise the water in the bath to a boiling heat. By looking at the engraving of the still, you will see what we mean. The inner boiler or concurbit, marked (2), is the vessel in which the liquids to be distilled are put, and the outer boiler or bath (A) is the vessel that should be filled with water. This is sometimes called a Bain Marie. The cover of the inner boiler must be well luted, that is, closed completely, to prevent evaporation. Take a lute, made of equal proportions of flour, whitening and salt, mixed together with the blade of a knife, and diluted with water; spread this on a piece of rag, and close all the crevices.

The object of distillation is to separate one substance from others with which it may be mixed. For example, in recipe No. 1, for making aqua de paradiso, or paradise water, 7 pints of alcohol, 95 per cent., and 20 pints of water, are distilled with a quantity of cocoa and spice. Now, as the alcohol distils at 176°, and water at 212°, it is perfectly apparent that the 7 pints of alcohol will all distil from off the water, and become impregnated with the flavor and taste of the cocoa and spices before the water begins to distil.

The greater the surface exposed, and the less the height the vapors have to ascend, the more rapidly does the distillation proceed; and so well are these principles understood by the Scotch distillers, that they do not take more than three minutes to discharge a still containing fifty gallons of fluid. The body of the still or boiler should never be filled above one-half, sometimes not above one fourth, to prevent the possibility of boiling or spirting over.

As a necessary appendage to the boiler, furnace, &c., a copper skimmer, with small holes, such as is used in kitchens, should be provided.

3. On Filtration.

The filtering Apparatus consists of a long, high, narrow, but strong table, in the middle of which are cut out round holes of 4 inches diameter, 2 feet distant from each other.

On the under part of the table around the holes are placed 4 hooks equidistant from each other, for hanging up the filtering-bags:

For filtering-bags, cut a yard of Canton flannel in three square pieces as exact as you can; double one of the square pieces, sew it on one side and let the other remain open, so that you form a triangle; the soft or cotton substance of the bag must form the inner side, with brass rings to hang the bag to the table sewed on. For every hole in the table there should be a correspondent filtering bag hung up. In connection with this process there must be provided as many pails as there are filterers in use ; for each pail there must be apportioned half of a sheet of blotting paper, prepared as follows: rub each piece of paper in your hands until it becomes smooth and pliant, as near to cloth as possible; then place it in the pail with a little water, constantly beating it and rubbing it together with the hands until it comes to the consistency of a soft or pulpy matter; afterward more water should be added, continuing the process of beating up the pulpy substance similar to the usual mode of beating up eggs; the pail must then be filled, and the contents thrown into the filterer. When the water has run through, fill up again so as to keep the filterer full, and when the water runs clear let the whole of the water pass through, and the bag is prepared to filter. Place a fiv-egallon demijohn under the filterer, with funnel, fill another demijohn with the liquor to be filtered; let the mouth of it, turned down, be placed (in the hole on the top of the table) in the bag, so that the neck of the demijohn will descend one inch in the filtering bag. The liquor from the upper demijohn will just fill the bag to the neck, the product of which will run clear, pure and bright into the demijohn below. In this way the distiller can employ as many filterers as he may desire, or produce as many different liquors as are wanted.

Spirits which are largely loaded with essential oils, such as those of anise-seed, &c., usually require the addition of a spoonful or two of magnesia before they will flow quite clear.

4. To Displace.

The kind of filtration commonly called the process of displacement, for extracting the essence from roots, herbs, seeds, barks, &c., is to be effected in the following manner: It is first necessary that the articles to be acted upon should be ground in a drug-mill to the condition of a coarse powder; then weigh each powder by itself, and mix them together in the proportions demanded by the recipe, and moisten the mass thoroughly with alcohol, allowing it to macerate* for twelve hours in a vessel well covered. Next you require a hollow instrument of cylindrical form, having one end shaped like a funnel, so that it can be inserted in the neck of a demijohn, and having inside, near the lower end, a partition pierced with numerous small holes, like the strainer of a French coffee-pot; in the absence of such a partition, soft cotton, or any insoluble substance, may be substituted, and being placed in the inside at the lower end of the instrument, will answer as well as the strainer. This instrument is called a percolator. Having let the ingredients be acted upon, macerate for the time we have named—introduce them into the percolator, and slightly press them upon the partition. Any portion of the liquid used in the maceration, not absorbed by the powder, should be poured upon the mass in the instrument, and allowed to percolate. You must now gradually pour into the percolator sufficient of the alcohol, or other liquid to be filtered, to drive before it, or displace, the liquid contained in the mass; the portion introduced must in like manner be displaced by another portion ; and so on, till you obtain the required quantity of filtered liquor. This extract is called tincture. In case the liquor which first passes through, should be thick and turbid, you must again introduce it into the instrument, and be very careful not to have the powder too coarse or loosely pressed, or it will permit the liquid to pass too quickly, and on the other hand it should not be too fine and compact, or it may offer an unnecessary resistance. Should the liquor flow too rapidly, you must return it to the instrument, and close it beneath for a time, and thus permit the finer parts of the powder to subside, and cause a slower percolation. If you have sufficient time, you can avoid the trouble of going through the process of displacement, by simply macerating the articles for two weeks, being careful to stir them up thoroughly once in every 24 hours.

* 5. Maceration is simply the immersing of certain substances in spirits or any other liquid, for a given length of time. By this process the strength and flavor are taken from the roots, seeds, &c, and imparted to the liquid. To macerate, the liquid should be at blood-heat.

6. On Clarification.

On the whole, clarification is preferable for syrups to filtration. They need only be beaten up while cold with a little white of egg, and then heated; a scum rises which must be removed as soon as it becomes consistent, and the skimming continued until the liquor becomes clear. Any floating portions of scum that may have escaped notice, are easily removed by running the syrup through a coarse flannel strainer whilst hot.

7. To Clarify Loaf-Sugar and make Syrup.

Take a copper pan, and put into it your sugar, broken in small pieces. The pan should be sufficiently large to allow the scum to rise a little without boiling over. One pint of water to every two pounds of sugar may be added. Beat up the whites of two eggs (if you are clarifying about ten pounds of sugar, or mix in this proportion), until it is very frothy, and then mix in with the rest. "Now place the pan on the fire, and have ready some cold water. When the mixture begins to boil and rise to the top of the pan, throw in a little of the water to prevent the sugar running over.

You must let the sugar rise three times before commencing to skim it, each time cooling the mixture by the cold water just spoken of. The fourth time the sugar rises, shim it completely, and drop the cold water gently in as occasion may require, continuing to take the scum* off (which is rather white), until no more comes upon the surface. The sugar must now be strained through a fine sieve—one made of cloth, or a flannel bag will do.

In order to make clarified sugar extra white, you must be careful to get the very best loaf-sugar. Break it up, as in the previous case, and add water in about the same proportion, viz., a pint to every two pounds, or two pounds and a half. Beat up well a couple of eggs (supposing ten pounds of sugar are being clarified) and add some ivory black, about a pound; see that the ivory-black is thoroughly mixed into the water. The mixture should now be made as hot as possible, but without being allowed to boil. If symptoms of boiling and rising appear, instantly add a drop of cold water. Having thoroughly melted the mixture, strain as before through a fine cloth, or flannel strainer. The syrup need not be heated any more, but it will have to be strained three or four times, until it is extra fine and clear.

* The scum need not be thrown away; after a quantity is collected, it can be clarified.

8. On Clarifying Brown or Moist Sugar.

Here, again, take care the pan is large enough to allow the syrup to rise without immediately boiling over. Brown sugar does not require so much water as loaf. A quart will be sufficient for five or six pounds of moist sugar. Thoroughly beat up one egg (the yolk had better be omitted, as it will only rise with the scum, and be skimmed off), and, as must be observed in the case of loaf-sugar, mix the egg in with the water before pouring it on the sugar. Now, get about one pound of charcoal (that made out of hedge wood, or small branches, is the best); beat it very fine, and stir it into the sugar. As it boils, skim it, as in the previous case, and add cold water to prevent it running over. Now commence straining it through a pocket shaped strainer of cloth. First of all it is quite black, but the straining must be proceeded with until the mixture is quite clear. If you pour some of the syrup into a glass, you will soon see if it is perfectly clear and fine, if it is not, you must keep on straining.

9. On the Degrees for Boiling Sugar.

You should have a perfect knowledge of the degrees of boiling sugar after it has been clarified. There are nine essential points, or degrees, in boiling sugar. They are called SMALL THREAD, LARGE THREAD, LITTLE PEARL, LARGE PEARL, THE BLOW, THE FEATHER, THE BALL, THE CRACK, THE CARAMEL.

10: The Small Thread.

The sugar being clarified, put it on the fire, and after boiling a few moments, gently dip the top of your forefinger into the syrup, and apply it to your thumb, when, on separating them immediately, the sugar forms a fine thread, which will break at a short distance, and remain as a drop on the finger and thumb. This is termed the "Small Thread."

11. The Large Thread.

Boil a little longer, and again dip the forefinger into the syrup, and apply it to the ball of the thumb. This time a somewhat longer string will be drawn. This is termed the "Large Thread."

12. The Little Pearl.

This is when you separate the thumb and finger, and the fine thread reaches, without breaking, from one to the other.

13. The Large Pearl.

When the finger and thumb are spread as far as possible, without the thread being broken, it is termed the "Large Pearl." Another sign, also, is sometimes shown, by the boiling syrup exhibiting bubbles on the surface. But this should be considered more as a hint than as a rule for guidance.

14. The Blow.

Continue boiling the syrup. Take your skimmer and dip it into the sugar, then shake it over the pan, hold it before you, and blow through the holes. If you perceive small bubbles, or little sparkling bladders, on the other side of the skimmer, these are signs that you have produced what is called the " Blow."

15. The Feather.

When you have boiled the mixture a little more, and again dipped the skimmer into it, and after shaking it, find, upon blowing through the holes, that bubbles are produced in much greater quantities, then you may be sure the "Feather" has been made. Another sign, after dipping the skimmer, is to shake it extra hard, in order to get off the sugar; if it has acquired this degree, you will see the melted sugar hanging from the skimmer like silk or flying flax; whence it is termed by the French la á grande plume.

16. The Ball.

To know when the "Ball" has been acquired, you must first dip the forefinger into a basin of cold water; now apply your finger to the syrup, taking up a little on the tip; then quickly dip it into the water again. If upon rolling the sugar with the thumb, you can make it into a small ball, you may be sure that what is termed the "Small Ball" has been produced. When you can make a larger and harder ball, which you could not bite without its adhering unpleasantly to the teeth, you may be satisfied that it is the "Large Ball."

17. The Crack.

Boil the syrup a very little more, dip the finger into the sugar, and if, upon taking it out, the sugar adhering to the finger breaks with a slight noise, and will not stick to the teeth when bitten, the " Crack" has been produced. Now boil the syrup up again, dip the finger into the cold water, then into the syrup, and as quickly into the water again. If the sugar breaks short and brittle upon doing this, it is the " Great Crack."

You cannot be too careful when the boiling syrup is at this degree, because it rapidly passes to what is termed the "Caramel." Be quick and cautious, as an additional stir of the fire, or one minute's delay, may cause the syrup to be scorched beyond cure.

18. The Caramel.

When the sugar has been boiled to the " Crack," as just stated, it quickly changes to the next degree. The syrup rapidly loses its whiteness, and begins to be slightly colored. You must now add to the syrup a few drops of lemon acid or juice, to prevent its graining. A little vinegar or a few drops of pyroligneous acid, will produce the desired effect.

Dropping the acid in is termed greasing it. Having given the syrup another slight boil, so as to assume a yellow color, take the pan from the fire and place it in a dish of cold water, two or three inches deep. This will prevent burning; a circumstance most to be feared in this process.

Unless care be used, it would soon turn from yellow to brown, and then to black. Especially be careful not to use too much acid or lemon-juice, for this will spoil the syrup, and probably produce the very graining you are trying to avoid. A small piece of butter put into the pan will prevent the syrup from rising over the sides, and will grease or smooth it, and thus act like the acid in keeping it from graining. A little cream of tartar also on the point of a knife, will prevent it from candying. All this time a good red fire (not a blaze) should be kept up underneath. A small piece of wet rag or flannel will keep the top edges of the pan from crusting with sugar, which might soon cake up and burn.

When boiling sugar, it is a good plan to keep the top somewhat covered after it has begun to boil, and before the syrup has been boiled to the "Crack." The steam by this plan is kept within; the sides are moistened, and no crust is formed.*

* If at any time you boil the syrup a little too much, or produce a degree beyond what you wish for, pour in a little water and boil it up again. Sugar that has been boiling too often loses many of its good qualities. Some sugars are not well adapted for boiling to the degrees, and no rules laid down would enable the practitioner to know when the "Crack" is near. Great care must, therefore, be used; and nothing but practice will enable you to be uniformly successful. It is an old axiom with confectioners and dealers in syrup, that " there are twenty ways to grease syrup, but none to make it grain when it is greasy."

With regard to the ninth degree of boiling sugar, the "Caramel," the name is derived from a Count Albufage Caramel, of Nismes, who discovered this stage of boiling.

19. Measures of the United States.

(Distilled Water.)

Measures of the
United States

1 gallon	8 pounds	2 halves
1/2 do	4 do	2 quarts
1 quart	2 do	4 pints
1 pint	1 do	4 gills
1/3 pint	1/3 do	2 gills

A large and a small pair of scales must be provided; the large for weighing sugar, &c., the smaller for drugs, &c., &c.

20. The weights are as follows:

1 pound   16 ounces

1/2 do	8 do
1/4 do	4 do
1 ounce	8 drachms
1 drachm	60 grains

All other articles and utensils, such as mortars, mills, funnels, demijohns, casks, bottles, labels, pumps, areometers, bung-hammers, bung-bores, boxes, cases, hammer and nails, and syphon, must be supplied, as necessary to the operations of distilling and preparing liquors, syrups, cordials, &c., &c.

RECIPES FOR TEN GALLONS EACH.

21. Aqua del Paradise (Water of Paradise.)

40 1/2 ounces of roast and ground cocoa.
6 2/3 do. ground cardamom seeds.
6 2/3 do. ground Ceylon cinnamon.
7 pints of alcohol, 95 per cent.
20 do. water.

Distil the 7 pints of alcohol from off the water and mix the 7 pints of flavored alcohol with 20 pints of alcohol, 95 per cent., then add slowly 53 pints of fine white simple syrup. (See Simple or Plain Syrup, No. 7.) Filter it if necessary. Color white.

22. Aqua Divina. (Divine Water.)

6 2/3 ounces of ground Ceylon cinnamon.
6 2/3 do. gum myrrh.
26 2/3 do. roasted cacao carac.
7 pints of alcohol, 95 per cent.
20 do. water.

Distil the 7 pints of alcohol from off the water, and mix the 7 pints of flavored alcohol with 20 pints of alcohol 95. per cent., then add alowly 53 pints of fine white plain syrup. (See Plain Syrup, No. 7.)

Filter if necessary. Color white.

23. Aqua Persicana. (Persicot Water.)

6 2/3 ounces of ground common cinnamon.

6 3/4 pounds of ground peach-kernels.

7 pints of alcohol.

20 pints of water.

Distil the 7 pints of alcohol from off the water, and mix the 7 pints of flavored alcohol with 20 pints of alcohol, 95 per cent., and 14 drops of otto of roses, then add slowly 53 pints of fine white plain syrup. (See Plain Syrup, No. 7.)

Filter if necessary. Color white.

24. Aqua Romana. (Water of Rome.)

6 2/3 ounces of ground Ceylon cinnamon.

6 2/3 do. do. aromatic calamus-root.

3 3/4 do. do. nutmegs.

7 pints of alcohol.

20 do. water.

Distil the 7 pints of alcohol from off the water, and mix the 2 pints of flavored alcohol with 20 pints of alcohol, 95 per cent., then add slowly 53 pints of fine white plain sugar syrup. (See Plain Syrup, No. 7.)

Filter if necessary. Color, white.

25. Ale, Table.

2 gallons of ground malt.

6 do. water, at 142° (degrees) heat.

Well stirred together; and let it stand for 1 1/2 hour, draw off the liquid as much as possible; repeat the same operation with 3 gallons more of the same warm water, and the same standing. Draw off the liquor again, and repeat the third time with 3 gallons more, as before; mix the liquors together, boil them with two ounces of hops. Clarify the whole with the white of an egg, filter while hot; cool it as quickly as possible, stir in 1/2 lb. of yeast, and let it ferment.

26. Ale, White Devonshire.
2 gallons of ground malt (barley).

1/2 lb. of hops.

2 lbs. of Grout's extract.

3/4 lb. of yeast.

12 gallons of water, at 142° (degrees) heat.

Manipulation as for table ale.

Grout's extract is made by mixing the malt (ground) with 2 lbs. of water, filling in a bottle covered, and letting it stand in a warm place until the fermentation has evaporated. The mixture to be of the consistence of an extract. After the fermentation is complete, and the ale settled, it is to be put in bottles and tied up.

27. Alkermes de Florence.
3 3/8 drachms of essence of vanilla.

23 drops of otto of roses.

Dissolved in 27 pints of alcohol, 95 per cent.; then boil for five minutes lbs. of figs, cut fine, in 53 pints of fine plain white syrup (see No. 7), and add the syrup to the alcohol.

Filter. Color rose with cochineal. (See No. 93.)

28. Amour Sans Fin. (Love without end.)
36 drops of otto of roses.

81 do. oil of Neroly.

108 do. oil of cloves. Dissolved in 27 pints of alcohol, 95 per cent.; add slowly 53 pints of fine plain white syrup. (See No. 7.)

Filter. Color rose with cochineal. (See No. 93.)

29. Angelica Brandy.
4 ounces of pimpinella root.

12 do. angelica do.

2 do. lavender flowers.

Ground and made a tincture, with one quart of alcohol, 95 per cent.; add the tincture to 4 gallons of the alcohol, and 6 gallons of water. Filter. Color pale brown with sugar-color. (See No. 88.)

30. Anise-seed Brandy.

2 1/2 drachms of oil of anise-seed.

1/2 do. do. star anise-seed.

Dissolved in 4 1/4 gallons of alcohol, 95 per cent.; then add 3/4 of a gallon of fine white plain syrup (see No. 7), mixed with 5 gallons of water. Filter. Color white.

31. Anise-seed Cordial.

3 drachms of oil of anise-seed.

Dissolved in 2 3/4 gallons of alcohol, 95 per cent.; then add 2 1/2 gallons of fine white syrup (see No. 7), mixed with gallons of water. Filter. Color white.

32. Anisette de Bordeaux.

2 1/2 lbs. of ground anise-seed.

2 1/4 ounces of ground coriander-seed.

7 do. do. Ceylon cinnamon.

7 pints of alcohol, 95 per cent.

20 do. water.

Distil the 7 pints of alcohol from off the water, and mix the 2 pints of flavored alcohol with 20 pints of alcohol, 95 per cent.; then add slowly 53 pints of fine white plain syrup. (See No. 7.) Filter, if necessary. Color white.

33. Anisette d'Hollande.

54 ounces of ground anise-seed.

27 do. do. star anise-seed.

7 pints of alcohol, 95 per cent.

20 do. water.

Distil the 7 pints of alcohol from off the water, and mix the t pints of flavored, alcohol with 26 pints of alcohol, 95 per cent.; then add slowly 47 pints of fine white plain syrup. (See No. 7.)

Filter. Color white.

34. Anisette de Martinique.

54 ounces of ground anise-seed.

13 1/2 do. do. star anise-seed.

7 pints of alcohol, 95 per cent.

20 do. water.

Distil the 7 pints of alcohol from off the water, and mix the 7 pints of flavored alcohol with 20 pints of alcohol, 95 per cent; then add slowly 53 pints of fine white plain syrup. (See No. 7.)

Filter, if necessary. Color white.

35. Anisette Fausse. (Imitation.)

26 1/2 ounces of ground anise-seed.

17 1/2 do. do. star anise-seed.

4 1/2 do. do. coriander-seed.

4 1/2 ounces of ground fennel-seed.

47 1/2 pints of alcohol 95 per cent.

27 do. water.

Distil the pints of alcohol from off the water, and mix the pints flavored alcohol with pints of fine white plain syrup. (See No. 7.)

Filter if necessary. Color white.

36. Arrack.

21 1/3 pints of fine Batavia arrack.

58 2/3 do. pure 4th proof rice spirit.

1/2 ounce oil of cocoa nuts.

Filter. Color white.

37. Beaume Humain. (Balsam of Man.)

23 drops of oil of roses.

54 do. do. cinnamon.

162 do. do. cedrat.

54 do. do. mace.

Dissolved in 27 pints of alcohol, 95 per cent., then add 53 pints of fine white plain syrup. (See No. 7.)

Filter. Color white.

38. Bishop.

100 grains of ground nutmegs.

60 do. do. white pepper,

1 1/4 ounce of cardamom seed,

1 1/2 do. mace.

20 pints of syrup (plain white, see No. 7).

60 do. claret wine.

Mixed and boiled together for 1 minute. Filtered.

39. Bishop Extract.

10 1/2 Lbs. of ground orange peel.

2 1/2 do. cinnamon.

2 1/2 do. cardamom.

10 gallons of alcohol, 95 per cent.

Macerate for 14 days (see No. 5); press, filter, color red with cochineal. (See No. 93.)

40. Bitters, Aromatic.

2 3/4 lbs. of ground dried small orange apples.

1/4 lb. do. orange peel.

2 ounces do. calamus root.

2 do. do. pimpinella root.

1 do. do. cut hops.

Macerate for 14 days with 10 gallons of spirit at 45 per cent. (see No. 5); press out the dregs, add 2£ pints of brown sugar syrup. (See Brown Syrup, No. 8.)

Filter. Color dark brown with coloring. (See No. 88.)

41. Bitter Danziger Drops. (See No. 144.)

2 ounces of ground centaurium.

3 do. do. angelica root.

3 1/2 drachms of aloes.

1 ounce of myrrh.

2 do. cassia flowers.

2 1/2 do. ginger.

1 1/2 do. nutmegs.

2 do. galanga root.

3/4 do. gentian do.

1 1/2 do. wormwood.

3/4 do. agaric, all coarse powdered.

Macerate for 14 days with 10 gallons of spirit at 45 per cent. proof (see No. 5); press out the dregs, filter, color dark brown with coloring. (See No. 88.)

42. Bitters, English.

3/4 lb. of lemon peels.

6 1/2 ounces of orange peels.

6 1/2 do. small orange apples.

1 1/2 ounce of calamus root.

1 1/2 do. angelica root.

1 1/2 do. galanga root.

3/4 do. quassia wood.

2 1/4 do. gentian root.

3 drachms of nutmegs.

3 do. cloves.

Ground to coarse powder; macerate with 4 1/2 gallons of alcohol, 95 per cent., for two weeks, or displace (see Nos. 4 and 5); add 4 1/4 lbs. of brown sugar, boiled, and clarified with 5 1/2 gallons of pure water (see No. 6); color it with 7 1/2 ounces of sugar coloring, dark brown. (See No. 88.) Filter.

43. Bitters, Essence.

1 7/8 lb. of orange peel.

1 7/8 lb. of orange apples.

1 7/8 lb. of gentian root.

1 7/8 lb. of lemon peel.

Ground to coarse powder; macerate or displace with gallons of alcohol, 95 per cent., mixed with gallons of water. Filter. (See Nos. 3, 4 and 5.)

44. Bitters, Hamburg.

2 ounces of agaric.

5 do. cinnamon.

4 do cassia buds.

1/2 do. grains of paradise.

8 do. quassia wood.

3/4 do. cardamom seed.

3 do. gentian root.

3 do. orange apples, dried.

1 1/2 do. orange peel.

Ground to coarse powder; macerate with 4 1/4 gallons of alcohol, 95 per cent. (see No. 5), mixed with 5 3/4 gallons of water; add 2 3/4 ounces of acetic aether.

Color brown. (See No. 88.)

45. Bitters, Orange.

6 lbs. of orange peel, macerate them for 24 hours with 1 gallon of water, cut the yellow part of the peel from off the white, and chop it fine; macerate with 4 3/4 gallons of alcohol, 95 per cent, for two weeks, or displace (see Nos. 4 and 5); then add a syrup made of 4 1/4 gallons of water and 16 lbs. of sugar. Filter. (See No. 3.)

46. Bitters, Spanish.

5 ounces of polypody.

6 do. calamus-root.

8 do. orris root.

2 1/2 do. coriander-seed.

1 do. centaurium.

3 do. orange peel.

2 do. German camomile flower.

Ground to coarse powder; macerate with 4 3/4 gallons of alcohol, 95 per cent. (see No. 5) ; then add 5 1/4 gallons of water, and 1 1/2 ounce of sugar.

Filter. Color brown. (See No. 88.)

47. Bitters, Stomach.

1/2 lb. of cardamom seed.

1/8 do. nutmegs.

1/4 do. grains of Paradise.

1/2 do. cinnamon.

1/4 do. cloves.

1/4 do. ginger.

1/4 lb. of galanga.

1/4 do. orange peel.

1/8 do. lemon peel.

Ground to coarse powder; macerate with 4 3/4 gallons of alcohol, 95 per cent. (see No. 5); then add a syrup made of gallons of 4 1/2 water, and 12 lbs. of sugar. (See No. 7.) Filter. (See No. 3.)

48. Bitters, Stoughton.

8 lbs. of gentian root.

6 do, orange peel,

1 1/2 do. snake root (Virginia).

1/2 do. American saffron.

1/2 do. red saunders wood.

Ground to coarse powder; displace with 10 gallons of 4th proof spirit. (See No. 4.)

49. Brandy, Angelica.

1 1/2 lb. of angelica root.

2 1/4 ounces of cinnamon.

1 1/2 do. lavender flowers.

1 1/2 do. liquorice-root.

Ground to coarse powder; then add to 10 gallons of proof spirit and 6 lbs. of rectifier's charcoal. Distil over to 50 per cent.; then mix 3 pints of white plain syrup (see No. 7), and so much of water as to get 10 gallons in the whole.

50. Brandy, Anise-seed.

3 lbs. of anise-seed.

2 ozs. of caraway seed.

3 ozs. of orris-root.

Ground to a coarse powder; then add to 10 gallons of proof spirit and 6 lbs. of rectifier's charcoal. Distil over to 50 per cent.; then mix 3 pints of white plain syrup (see No. 7), and as much water as to get 10 gallons.

51. Brandy, Blackberry.

1/2 ounce of cinnamon.

1/4 do. cloves,

1/4 do. mace,

1/8 do. cardamom.

Ground to a coarse powder; add to 16 lbs. of blackberries, mashed, and 5 gallons of alcohol, 95 per cent. Macerate for two weeks (see No. 5); press it; then add 10 lbs. of sugar, dissolved in 3⅜ gallons of water. Filter, (see No. 3).

52. Brandy, British.

1 ounce of catechu,

1/2 drachm of vanilla, finely powdered.

Add 1 gallon of fine good Cognac and 9 gallons of pure proof spirit. Color pale or dark (see No. 88.)

53. Brandy, Calamus.

1/2 drachm of oil of lemon.

1/2 ounce of oil of calamus.

5 drops oil of coriander.

Dissolve in 4 3/4 gallons of alcohol, 95 per cent.; then add 5 gallons of water, and 1/4 gallon white plain syrup (see No. 7). Flesh-color with tincture of saffron and cochineal (see Nos. 91 and 93).

54. Brandy, Carminative.

1 1/2 drachms of oil of calamus.

16 drops of oil of anise-seed.

32 do. do. orange.

16 drops of oil of coriander.

16 do. do. lemon balm.

Dissolve in 4 3/4 gallons of alcohol, 95 per cent.; then add 5 gallons of water and 1/4 gallon white plain syrup (see No. 7). Color yellow (see No. 91).

55. Brandy, Caraway.

1 ounce of oil of caraway-seed.

30 drops of oil of anise-seed.

5 drops of oil of coriander-seed.

Dissolved in 4 3/4 gallons of alcohol, 95 per cent.; then add 5 gallons of water and gallon of white plain syrup (see No. 2).

56. Brandy, Cherry.

16 lbs. of black cherries, mashed with the stones.

5 gallons of alcohol, 95 per cent.

Macerate for two weeks (see No. 5); press it; then add 10 lbs. of sugar, dissolved in 3 3/8 gallons of water. Filter (see No. 3).

57. Brandy, Cinnamon.

1/2 ounce of oil of cinnamon.

32 drops of oil of cassia-buds.

32 do. oil of cloves.

Dissolve in 4 3/4 gallons of alcohol, 95 per cent.; then add 4 3/4 gallons of water and 1/2 gallon of white plain syrup (see No. 7). Color brown (see No. 88).

58. Brandy, Cloves.
4 1/2 drachms of oil of cloves,

1/2 drachm of oil of cinnamon.

Dissolve in 4 3/4 gallons of alcohol, 95 per cent.; then add 4 3/4 gallons of water and 1/2 gallon of white plain syrup (see No. 7). Color dark-brown (see No. 88).

59. Brandy, Domestic.
50 drops of oil of Cognac.

3 drachms of orris-root powder.

1 drachm of finely-cut vanilla.

Macerate in 4 ounces of alcohol, 95 per cent,, in a warm place, for 24 hours (see No. 5); filter, and then add to it 9 3/4 gallons of fourth-proof spirit (purest quality), and 1½, pints of white plain syrup (see No. 7). Color pale or dark with coloring (see No. 88).

60. Brandy, French.
1 gallon of genuine Otard brandy.

8 7/8 gallons of fourth-proof spirit (pure).

1/8 gallon of pure white plain syrup (see No. 7). Color dark or pale with coloring (see No. 88).

61. Brandy, Ginger.
1/2 lb. of white ginger, cut and washed.

7 1/2 lbs. of sugar, boiled for ten minutes with 3 gallons of water; strain; then add 2 gallons of fourth-proof spirit. Color pale yellow (see No. 91).

62. Brandy, Grunewald.
1/4 lb. of orange peel.

1/4 lb. of centaurium.

1 oz. of ginger. ,

1 1/3 oz. of calamus-root.

1 1/3 do. blessed thistle.

1 oz. of wormwood.

2/3 do. trefolii.

1 1/3 drachm of oil of cloves.

1 1/3 do. oil of cinnamon.

2/3 do. oil of peppermint.

4 3/4 gallons of alcohol, 95 per cent.

Macerate for 24 hours (see No. 5); then add to the strained and filtered tincture a syrup made of 3/4 gallon of white plain syrup (see No. 7), dissolved in 4 1/2 gallons of water. Color brown. (See No. 88.)

63. Brandy, Imperial Peach.

4 1/2 ozs. of powdered bitter almonds.

3 3/4 gallons of alcohol, 95 per cent.

5 1/4 gallons water.

Mix together, and macerate for 24 hours (see No. 5); then add a strained syrup, made of 3 3/4 lbs. of sugar; 1 pint of peach jelly; 2 1/4 ozs. preserved ginger; 1 lemon, cut in slices; 1 drachm of grated nutmegs; 1 drachm of allspice, in powder, and 5 pints of water, boiled for two minutes. Mix the whole, and filter.

64. Brandy, Juniper.

9 drachms of best oil of juniper, dissolved in

4 3/4 gallons of alcohol, 95 per cent.;

then add 6 lbs. of sugar, dissolved in 4 7/8 gallons of water. Filter.

65. Brandy, Mint.

1/2 ounce of oil of spearmint.

30 drops of oil of peppermint.

3 drops of oil of bergamot.

Dissolve in 4 3/4 gallons of alcohol 95 per cent., then add 3 lbs. of sugar dissolved in 5 1/3 gallons of water.

Color green with indigo and saffron tincture. (See No. 90.)

66. Brandy, Orange.

4 1/2 drachms of oil of orange.

3 drops of oil of neroly.

Dissolve in 4 3/4 gallons of alcohol 95 per cent., then add 2 1/2 lbs. of sugar dissolved in 5 1/8 gallons of water. Filter. (See No. 3.)

67. Brandy, Peach.

18 lbs. of peaches mashed with the stones, macerate them for 24 hours with 4 3/4 gallons of alcohol, 95 per cent. (see No. 5), and 4 gallons of water.

Strain, press, and filter; add 5 pints of white plain syrup. (See No. 7.)
Color dark yellow with coloring. (See No. 88.)

68. Brandy, Peppermint.

1/2 ounce of oil of peppermint (English).

Dissolve in 4 3/4 gallons of alcohol, 95 per cent., then add
4 3/4 lbs of sugar dissolved in 5 gallons of water. Filter. (See No. 3.)

69. Brandy, Raspberry.

4 gallons of raspberry juice, 4 3/4 gallons of alcohol, 95 per cent., macerate for 2 days (see No. 5), then add 1 1/4 gallon of white plain syrup (see No. 7). Filter.

70. Brandy, Spice.

2 1/2 ounces of cinnamon.

3/4 do. cloves.

3/4 do. cardamom.

1 do. galanga root.

1 do. ginger.

Ground to a coarse powder; macerate it for a week with 10 gallons of good French brandy. (See No. 5). Filter.

71. Brandy, Stomach. (Green.)

1/4 lb. of cubebs.

2 1/2 ounces of centaurium.

1 1/4 do. trefolii.

2 do. cassia buds.

Ground to coarse powder; macerate for one week in 4 3/4 gallons of alcohol, 95 percent. (See No. 5.) Filter, then add

1/2 drachm of oil of rosemary.

1/2 do. oil of sage.

1/2 do. oil of camomile.

1/2 do. oil of peppermint.

1/2 do. oil of spearmint.

1/2 do. oil of lavender.

1/2 do. oil of caraway.

1/4 do. oil of origanum.

1/4 do. oil of lemon.

1/4 do. oil of coriander-seed.

1/4 do. oil of anise-seed.

3/8 do. oil of fennel-seed.

After being dissolved, add 4 lbs. of sugar dissolved in 5 gallons of water. Color green with tincture of indigo and saffron. (See No. 90.)

72. Brandy, Stomach. (White.)

1/4 drachm of oil of anise-seed.

1/2 do. oil of coriander seed.

1/2 do. oil of spearmint.

1 do. oil of orange.

1/4 do. oil of cloves.

1/4 do. oil of cinnamon.

2 do. oil of calamus.

Dissolve in 4 3/4 gallons of alcohol, 95 per cent.; mixed with 4 lbs. of sugar, dissolved in 5 gallons of water. Filter. (See No. 3.)

73. Brandy, Strawberry.

4 gallons of strawberry juice.

4 3/4 gallon of alcohol, 95 per cent.
Macerate for 2 days (see No. 5), then add gallons of plain white syrup.
(See No. 7.) Filter. (See No. 3.)

74. Brandy, "Wormwood.

2 1/2 drachms of oil of wormwood.
1 1/4 ounces of herb of wormwood.
3/4 do. calamus root.
The herb and root must be ground and macerated (see No. 5) a few days,
then pressed, and the oil dissolved in 4 3/4 gallons of alcohol, 95 per cent.;
add a syrup made of 4 lbs. of sugar, with 5 gallons of water. Filter, and
color green, with tincture of Indigo and saffron. (See No. 90.)

75. Calabre à chaud.

36 gallons of white or red wine must, boiled and skimmed down to 8 3/4
gallons; to this add 1 1/4 gallon of alcohol, 95 per cent.
Use: for manufacture of Malaga wine.

76. Calabre à froid.

9 gallons of fresh, pure red or white wine must.
1 gallon of alcohol, 95 per cent.
Let it clarify itself by standing. Decant.
Use: For the manufacture of different wines.

77. Canelin de Corfou.

2 drachms of oil of Ceylon cinnamon.
Dissolve in 3 1/3 gallons of alcohol, 95 per cent.; then add 6 2/3 gallons of
white plain syrup. (See No. 7.) Color, yellow. (See No. 91.)

78. Canelle.

6 3/4 drachms of oil of cinnamon.
Dissolve in 3 1/3 gallons of alcohol, 95 per cent.; then add 6 2/3 gallons of
plain white syrup. (See No. 7.)

79. Cedrat.

13 1/2drachms of oil of cedar.

Dissolve in 3 1/3 gallons of alcohol, 95 per cent., and 6 2/3 gallons of white plain syrup. (See No. 7.) Color, yellow. (See No. 91.)

80. Champ d'Asile.

8 ounces of caraway-seed.

4 do. grains d'ambrette.

1 1/3 do. Ceylon cinnamon, ground to coarse powder; macerate and distil with 3 gallons of alcohol, 95 per cent, and 3 1/2 gallons of water.

Distil the 3 gallons of alcohol from off the water, and mix the 3 gallons of aromatic spirit with a syrup made of 42 lbs. of sugar and 43/4 gallons of water. (See No. 7.) Filter. .

81. Christine.

2 drachms of essence of vanilla.

8 drops of oil of roses.

24 do. oil of neroly.

48 do. oil of cinnamon.

Dissolve in 3 gallons of 95 per cent. alcohol; mix it with a syrup made of 42 lbs. of sugar, and 4 3/4 gallons of water. (See No. 7.)

82. Christophelet.

6 4/5 drachms of Spanish saffron.

14 1/5 do. cinnamon.

6 4/5 do. cardamom.

10 1/5 ounces of figs.

10 1/5 drachms of galanga-root.

4 1/4 ounces of orris-root.

2 1/2 do. sage.

4 1/4 do. staranis.

2 1/8 do. coriander-seed.

Ground to a coarse powder. Macerate (see No. 5), and distil with 6 gallons of alcohol, 95 per cent., and 1 1/4 gallons of water. Distil off 5 gallons of the aromatic spirit; then add 1 1/4 gallons of St. Julien Medoc wine; 1 1/4 gallons of distilled water; 13 drops of tincture of ambergris, and 2 1/2 gallons of white plain syrup (see No. 7). Color purple with tincture of elderberry (see No. 92).

83. Cider, Champagne.

10 gallons of cider, old and clear.
Put it in a strong iron-bound casks, pitched inside (like beer-casks); add 2 1/2 pints clarified white plain syrup (see No. 7); dissolve in it 5 ounces of tartaric acid. Keep the bung ready in hand; then add 7 1/2 ounces of bicarbonate of potassa; bung it as quickly, and well as possible.

84. Cider, Strong.

Take as many apples as will make juice sufficient to fill a strong cask. Make a pulp of them, by passing them through a cider-mill. Spread this pulp out on a large surface, in the open air, and leave it for 24 hours. Press out the juice as thoroughly as possible, and fill the cask up to the bung-hole, and keep it full as long as the fermentation is going on, by adding some juice kept aside for that purpose. When the fermentation is ended, draw it off in another clean cask; but previous to filling this cask, burn 1 drachm of brimstone in it, by hanging an iron vessel through the bung-hole. Bung it up carefully, and keep it in a cool place.

85. Cider, Sweet.

Procure a cask, pitched inside (like a beer-cask); then take as many sweet apples as will make juice sufficient to fill it. Press the apples as quickly as possible, being careful to let the juices settle a little while; then decant the juice, and put it in the cask in the following manner, viz.: 1st. Burn 1/2 ounce of brimstone in the cask (as described in recipe No. 84). 2d. Bung up the cask and let it stand a while. 3d. Fill the cask 1/3 full with the juice, being very careful to shake it well. Go through this process three times, and be very particular to observe the above directions each time. After you have put the last 1/3 of the juice in the cask, bung it carefully, and put it in a cool place for use.

86. Citron.

1 ounce of oil of lemon, dissolved in
3 1/3 gallons of alcohol, 95 per cent.
Then add gallons of white plain syrup (see No. 7). Color yellow (see No. 91).

87. Citronelle.

1 lb. of lemon peel, only the yellow part.
2 ounces of orange peel, only the yellow part.
1 drachm of cloves.
1 do. nutmegs. Cut in small pieces; macerate with 5 gallons of alcohol, 95 per cent., and 5 gallons of water (see No. 5). Distil off 8 gallons of aromatic spirit, and mix it with 2 gallons of white plain syrup (see No. 7). Color yellow (see No. 91).

88. Coloring.

Take 100 lbs. of white sugar, and mix with it 3 gallons of water, in a copper or iron boiler of 50 gallons capacity. It is necessary to have the boiler this size, as in manufacturing coloring the liquid is apt to run over when made in a smaller vessel. Put the boiler on a smart fire, and stir the sugar constantly, so as to prevent its burning on the bottom. Keep it boiling until it gets as black as tar when dropped on a cold stone.. Then add slowly 6 1/4 gallons of boiling water—at first, only a little at a time, and increasing the quantity gradually—constantly stirring as the whole is dissolved. Pass it through a flannel.

89. Color, Blue.

Take 3 ounces of sulphuric acid (smoking) and put it in a one-gallon glass jar; add, in very small portions, 1 ounce of the finest powdered indigo, being very careful to stir the ingredients constantly during the process of mixing them. Let the jar stand in a warm place for several days, and then add, very slowly, 3 quarts of water; after which add, in small quantities, 1/2 lb. of chalk powder, and continue stirring it as long as a froth rises from the mixture. After having done this, let it stand for 24 hours, then decant, filter, mix 1 1/2 pint of alcohol with it, and bottle for use.

90. Color, Green.

By mixing the tincture of saffron and the tincture of indigo together in different proportions, you can obtain any shade of green you desire. For a light-green, increase the saffron; for a dark-green increase the indigo.

91. Color, Yellow.

Mix 1/4 lb. American saffron, cut very fine, with 1 quart of alcohol, 95 per cent.; put it in a covered jar, in a warm place, and let it stand for 8 days; then press, filter, and bottle for use. A yellow coloring may also be made of turmeric instead of saffron. Observe the same proportions, and make in the same way.

92. Color, Purple.

Mix 1/2 lb. elderberries, mashed to a pulp, with 1 quart of of alcohol, 95 per cent. Macerate (see No. 5) in a warm place for 8 days; then press, filter, and bottle for use.

93. Color, Red.

1 ounce of finely-powdered cochineal.
1/2 drachm of calcinated alum.
Boiled with a quart of water, in an earthen dish; add 1 quart of alcohol, 95 per cent., press, filter, and bottle for use.

94. Color, Violet.

1 pint of blue color.
2 pints of red color.
Mix together.

95. Coquette Flatteuse.

24 drops of oil of rose.

48 do. oil of mace.

32 do. essence of ambergris.

Dissolve in 3 gallons of alcohol, 95 per cent.; then add a syrup made of 42 lbs. of sugar and 4 3/4 gallons of water (see No. 7). Color rose (see No. 93).

96. Cordial.

32 drops of oil of cinnamon.

24 do. oil of cloves.

24 do. oil of mace.

48 do. oil of peppermint.

Dissolve in 3 gallons of alcohol, 95 per cent.; add a syrup made of 42 lbs. of sugar and 4 3/4 gallons of water (see No. 7). Filter (see No. 3).

97. Cordial, Bright Pearl. (Jelly.)

2 ounces of candied lemons.

2 do. lemon peel.

3 do. candied ginger.

4 do. raw ginger.

Boil for 20 minutes in 2 gallons of water, strain it, and add to the strained liquor a jelly made of the following ingredients.

4 ounces of currant jelly.

2 do. almonds blanched and broken.

1 do. almond bitter, " " "

2 do. St John's bread, broken and mashed.

1 do. conserve of white roses.

1 do. ginger powdered.

1 do. cinnamon "

1 do. mace.

1/2 pint of lemon juice, 7 gallons of fourth-proof spirit, 2 ounces of isinglass dissolved in water; put this together in a stone pot well covered; then take 6 lbs. of Malaga raisins boiled with one gallon of water, and mix with the above; press and filter it through a flannel while hot.

98. Cordial, Caraway.

6 drachms of oil of caraway dissolved in 3 gallons of alcohol, 95 per cent.; add a syrup made of 42 lbs. of sugar and 4 3/4 gallons of water. (See No. 7). Filter.

99. Cordial, Cherry.

30 lbs. of cherries, red sour, without stems, make them to a pulp and macerate with 4 1/2 gallons of alcohol, 95 per cent. (see No. 5); press, and add a syrup made of 42 lbs. of sugar and 3 1/2 gallons of water. (See No. 7.) Filter.

100. Cordial, Cinnamon.

1/2 ounce of oil of cinnamon, dissolved in 3 gallons of alcohol, 95 per cent; then add a syrup made of 42 lbs. of sugar, and 3 1/2 gallons of water. (See No. 7.) Filter.

101. Cordial, Cloves.

12 ounces of cloves.

3 do. orris-root.

2 do. cinnamon.

1/2 do. cardamom.

Ground to coarse powder; macerate or displace with 5 1/2 gallons of alcohol, 95 per cent. (see Nos. 4 and 5), and 5 1/2 gallons of water. Distil from off the water 5 gallons of aromatic spirit, and then add a syrup made of 24 lbs. of sugar and 3 1/2 gallons of water. (See No. 7).

Color brown with tincture of cloves.

102. Cordial, Ginger.

10 ounces of ground ginger, 5 drops of oil of bergamot; macerate it with 3 gallons of alcohol 95 per cent., press and filter, and then add a syrup made with 42 lbs. of sugar, and 4 3/4 gallons of water. (See No. 7). Color pale yellow. (See No. 91.)

Red ginger is the same as the above, except it is colored red with cochineal.

103. Cordial, Green Gage.

8 lbs. of ripe gages and 42 lbs. of sugar, 4 3/4 gallons of water; boil them tender and make them to a pulp, skim and take from the fire, then add:

4 ounces of currant jelly.

4 do. dates, cut in small pieces.

4 do. ounces of figs, do. do.

1/2 pint of orange juice.

3 do. sherry wine.

1 do. calf's-foot jelly.

1 ounce of candied lemon.

1 do. cinnamon.

1 do. cloves.

2 do. ginger.

1 do. nutmeg.

1 do. pimento.

All coarsely powdered; macerate for one week (see No. 5), and add 2 gallons of alcohol, 95 per cent.; strain, press and filter.

104. Cordial, Lemon.

2 lbs. of fresh lemon peel.

1/4 do. roasted wheat bread, crusts,

1/4 do. cinnamon, crushed.

1/2 ounce of nutmeg, do.

Cut small and macerate for one week with 5 1/2 gallons of alcohol, 95 per cent., and 5 1/2 gallons of water.

Distil from off the water 5 gallons of aromatic spirit, and add to this 30 drops of oil of lemon, and a syrup made of 24 lbs. of sugar, and 3 1/2 gallons of water. (See No. 7.)

Color, pale yellow. (See No. 91.)

105. Cordial, Maccaron, French.

22 ounces of bitter almonds.

1 1/2 do. cinnamon.

1 1/2 do. cloves,

1 1/2 do. cardamom.

Ground to coarse powder; macerate for one week, with 5 1/2 gallons of alcohol, 95 per cent., and 5 1/2 gallons of water.

Distil from off the water 5 gallons of aromatic spirit, and mix it with a syrup made of 24 lbs. of sugar, and gallons of water. (See No. 7.) Filter.

106. Cordial, Mint.

1/2 ounce of oil of spearmint.

Dissolve in 3 gallons of alcohol, 95 per cent., then add a syrup made of 42 lbs. of sugar and 4 3/4 gallons of water. (See No. 7.)

Color green, with tincture of indigo and saffron. (See No. 90.)

107. Cordial, Noyau.

1 1/4 lb. of apricot kernels.

1/2 do. peach do.

1/2 do. prune do.

The rinds of 12 oranges, cut in small pieces. Macerate for 24 hours in 3 1/2 gallons of alcohol, 95 per cent., and 3 1/2 gallons of water.

Distil from off the water 3 gallons of flavored spirit, and mix it with a syrup made of 42 lbs. of sugar, and 4 3/4 gallons of water. (See No. 7.) Filter.

108. Cordial, Orange.

1 ounce of oil of orange.

Dissolve in 3 gallons of alcohol, 95 per cent., then add a syrup made of 42 lbs. of sugar, and 4 3/4 gallons of water. (See No. 7.)

Color yellow, with a tincture of saffron. (See No. 91.)

109. Cordial, Peach.

12 lbs. of peaches and kernels mashed to a pulp; let them ferment for eight days, and then boil for 2 minutes in 2 gallons of white plain syrup. (See No. 7.) Strain, then add 3 gallons of alcohol, 95 per cent. Color yellow, and filter. (See No. 91.)

110. Cordial, Peppermint,

1/2 ounce of oil peppermint dissolved in 3 gallons of alcohol 95 per cent.; add 7 gallons of white plain syrup. (See No. 7.) Filter.

111. Cordial Persicot.

3 lbs. of peach kernels.

6 ounces of lemon peel.

2 do. cinnamon .

1/2 do. cloves.

1/2 do. nutmegs

Macerate for 24 hours in 3 1/2 gallons of alcohol, 95 per cent., and 3 1/2 gallons of water. Distil from off the water 3 gallons of flavored spirit, then add 7 gallons of white plain syrup. (See No. 7.)

Color peach-blossom color, with tincture of cochineal. (See No. 93.)

112. Cordial, Quince.

48 ounces of quinces, grated, macerate for 8 days in 3 1/2 gallons of alcohol 95 per cent., and 3 1/2 gallons of water. Distil from off the water, 3 gallons of flavored spirit, add 2 gallons of white plain syrup. (See No. 7.)

113. Cordial Railroad.

2 drachms of oil of peppermint.

1 do. do. wormwood.

32 drops of oil of roses.

1 drachm of oil of hyssop.

Dissolve in 3 gallons of alcohol 95 per cent., then add 7 gallons of white plain syrup. (See No. 7.)

Color lilac. (See No. 94.)

114. Cordial Raspberry.

12 lbs. of raspberries; boil the juice with 6 1/2 gallons of white plain syrup (see No. 7); add 3 gallons of alcohol 95 per cent. Filter.

115. Cordial Red "Water.

1 ounce of cloves.

1 do. cinnamon.

1 do. Jamaica pepper.

1 do. nutmegs; all ground to a coarse powder.

Macerate for 8 days in 3 gallons of alcohol, 95 per cent. (see No. 5); add 7 gallons of white plain syrup. (See No. 7.) Color red with cochineal. (See No. 93.) Filter.

116. Cordial, Rose.

40 drops of oil of roses.

40 do. tincture of musk.

24 do. oil of orange.

Dissolve in 3 gallons of alcohol, 95 per cent., then add 7 gallons of white plain syrup. (See No. 7.)

Color rose with cochineal. (See No. 93.)

117. Cordial, Celery.

1 lb. of celery seed, and 5 lbs. of celery root, boiled for 2 minutes with 7 gallons of white plain syrup (see No. 7), then add 3 gallons of alcohol, 95 per cent., strain, filter ; color with tincture of turmeric. (See No. 91).

118. Cordial Smallage.

3 lbs. of raisins, seeded, 5 lbs. of young sprouts of smallage; cut and wash them; boil for 2 minutes in 7 gallons of white plain syrup (see No. 7); strain, then add 3 gallons of alcohol, 95 per cent. Filter.

119. Creme d'Absinthe. (Absinthe Cream.)

24 ounces of wormwood and 8 ounces of anise-seed finely ground Macerate for 24 hours in 3 1/2 gallons of alcohol, 95 per cent., and 3 2/3 gallons of water. Distil from off the water 3 1/2 gallons of flavored spirit, and then add a syrup made of 53 lbs. of sugar and 3 1/4 gallons of water, near boiling heat. (See No. 7.)
Color green with indigo and saffron. (See No. 90.)

120. Creme d'Angelique. (Angelica Cream.)

12 ounces of angelica root powdered ; macerate for 24 hours in 3 2/3 gallons of alcohol 95 per cent. (see No. 5), add 2 2/3 gallons of water. Distil over 3 1/3 gallons of flavored spirit; then add 53 lbs. of sugar, and 3 1/4 gallons of alcohol near boiling heat.

121. Creme d'Anise. (Anise-seed Cream.)

24 ounces of green anise-seed.

8 do. star anise-seed.

4 do. cinnamon.

Ground; then macerate for 24 hours in 3 1/8 gallons of alcohol, 95 per cent., and 3 2/3 gallons of water; distil from off the water 3 1/3 gallons of flavored spirit, then add 53 lbs. of sugar and 3 1/4 gallons of water, near boiling heat.

122. Creme de Barbadoes. (Barbadoes Cream.)

4 lemons, the rinds only.

4 oranges, Ceylon,

5 1/3 do. ounces of cinnamon.

3 drachms of mace.

1 1/2 drachms of cloves.

11 do. coriander-seed.

11 do. bitter almonds.

1 1/2 do. nutmegs.

Ground and cut; macerate for 24 hours in 3 1/2 gallons of alcohol, 95 per cent., and 3 2/3 gallons of water. Distil from off the water 3 1/3 gallons of flavored spirit; then add 53 lbs. of sugar, and 3 1/4 gallons of water, near boiling heat.

123. Creme de Cacao. (Cocoa Cream.)

5 lbs. of roasted cacao.

1 ounce of Ceylon cinnamon.

Ground; macerate for 24 hours in 3 1/2 gallons of alcohol, 95 per cent., and 3 2/3 gallons of water. Distil from off the water 3 1/3 gallons of flavored spirit, then add 53 lbs. of sugar and 3 1/4 gallons of water, near boiling heat; add one ounce of tincture of vanilla.

124. Creme de Cedrat with Champagne. (Cedrat Cream.)

1 ounce of oil of cedrat, dissolve in 2 1/3 gallons of alcohol, 95 per cent., add 4 quart bottles of champagne, 53 lbs. of sugar, and 3 1/4 gallons of water, near boiling heat.

125. Creme de Chocolat. (Chocolate Cream.)

8 lbs. of roasted cacao.

12 ounces of cinnamon.

4 do. vanilla.

1/2 do. cloves.

Ground; macerate for 48 hours in 3 1/3 gallons of alcohol, 95 per cent., 3 2/3 gallons of water. (See No. 5.) Distil from off the water 3 1/3 gallons of high-flavored spirit; then add 53 lbs. of sugar, and 3 1/4 gallons of water, near boiling heat.

126. Creme de Cinnamon.

(Cinnamon Cream.)

162 drops of oil of cinnamon.

Dissolve in 3 1/3 gallons of alcohol, 95 per cent.; then add 53 lbs. of sugar, and gallons of water, near boiling heat.

Color yellow. (See No. 91.)

127. Creme de Cinq Fruits. (Cream of Five Fruits)

6 bergamots, the rinds only.

6 bitter oranges, do. do.

6 cedrats, do. do.

6 lemons, do. do.

9 oranges, do. do.

Cut small; macerate for 24 hours with 3 1/3 gallons of alcohol, 95 per cent., and 3 2/3 gallons of water (see No. 5).

Distil from off the water gallons of flavored spirit, then add 53 lbs. of sugar and gallons of water, near boiling heat.

128, Creme de Dattes. (Date Cream.)

8 lbs. of dates pounded, and boiled with 53 lbs. of sugar, 3 1/4 gallons of water; strain and press; then add 72 drops of oil of neroly, and dissolve in 3 1/3 gallons of alcohol, 95 per cent.

129. Creme Imperiale. (Imperial Cream.)

4 ounces of carrot-seed.

4 do. Ceylon cinnamon.

8 do. angelica-seed.

8 do. orris-root.

Ground; macerate for 24 hours with 3 1/3 gallons of alcohol, 95 per cent., and 3 2/3 gallons of water. (See No. 5.) Distil from off the water 3 1/3 gallons of flavored spirit; then add 53 lbs of sugar and 3 1/4 gallons of water, heated near boiling.

130. Creme de Martinique. (Martinique Cream.)

4 drachms of tincture of vanilla.

32 drops of oil of neroly.

14 drops of oil of roses.

24 drops of oil of cinnamon.

Dissolve in 3 1/3 gallons of alcohol, 95 per cent.; then add 53 lbs. of sugar and gallons of water, near boiling heat, and color rose. (See No. 93.)

131. Creme de Menthe. (Mint Cream.)

5 lbs. of spearmint.

25 lemons, the rinds only.

Cut and macerate for 24 hours with 3 1/3 gallons of alcohol, 95 per cent., and 3 2/3 gallons of water. (See No. 5.) Distil from off the 3 1/3 water gallons of flavored spirit, and dissolve in it 5 drachms of oil of peppermint; then add 53 lbs. of sugar and 3 1/4 gallons of water, near boiling heat.

132. Creme de Mocha. (Coffee Cream)

32 ounces of Mocha coffee roasted and ground, macerate for 24 hours with 3 1/3 gallons of alcohol, 95 per cent., add 3 2/3 gallons of water (see No. 5). Distil from off the water 3 1/3 gallons of flavored spirit, and dissolve in it one drachm of essence of vanilla, then add 53 lbs. of sugar and 3 1/4 gallons of water near boiling heat.

133. Creme de Nymphe. (Lady's Cream.)

97 drops of oil of cinnamon.

49 do. oil of mace.

24 do. oil of roses.

Dissolve in gallons of alcohol, 95 per cent., then add 53 lbs. of sugar and gallons of water, near boiling heat. Color rose. (See No. 93.)

134. Creme d'Orange, with Champagne. (Orange Cream.)

1 ounce of oil of orange, dissolve in 2 1/3 gallons of alcohol, 95 per cent., add 4 quart bottles of champagne, 53 lbs. of sugar, and 3 1/4 gallons of water, near boiling heat.

135. Creme de Portugal. (Portugal Cream.)

1 ounce of oil of Portugal; dissolve in 3 1/3 gallons of alcohol, 95 per cent., add 53 lbs. of sugar and 3 1/4 gallons of water, near boiling heat.

136. Creme de Roses. (Rose Cream.)

Dissolve 1 drachm of oil of roses, in 3 1/2 gallons of alcohol, 95 per cent., then add 53 lbs. of sugar and 3 1/4 gallons of water near boiling heat, and color rose. (See No. 93.)

137. Creme Royale. (Royal Cream.)

4 ounces of cloves.

4 do. cinnamon.

8 do. carrot-seed.

10 oranges, the rinds only.

Macerate for 24 hours with 3 1/3 gallons of alcohol, 95 per cent., and 3 2/3 gallons of water (see No. 5). Distil from off the water 3 1/3 gallons of flavored spirit, then add 53 lbs. of sugar and 3 1/4 gallons of water near boiling heat.

138. Creme de Truffles. (Cream of Truffles.)

1 lb. of truffles, ground; macerate for 8 days with 3 1/3 gallons of alcohol, 95 per cent. (see No. 5); strain, press and add 53 lbs. of sugar, and 3 1/4 gallons of water, near boiling heat.

Color dark yellow. (See No. 88).

139. Creme de Vanille. (Vanilla Cream Cordial.)

2 drachms of vanilla bean, cut fine ; macerate for 2 days in 3 1/2 gallons of alcohol, 95 per cent. (see No. 5); then add 53 lbs. of sugar and 3 1/4 gallons of water, near boiling heat.

140. Creme Virginal. (Virgin's Cream.)

1 5/8 gallons of rose-water.

1 5/8 do. orange-flower water.

Dissolve in it 53 lbs. of sugar, then add 3 1/3 gallons of alcohol, 95 per cent. Filter.

141. Cuckold's Comfort.

4 1/2 lbs. of fresh poppies mashed, macerate one week with 4 gallons of proof spirit (see No. 5); strain, press, add one gallon of white plain syrup (see No. 7); flavor with 1/2 ounce of essence of vanilla, 24 drops of oil of roses, dissolve in 2 ounces of alcohol, 95 per cent. Filter. (See No. 3.)

142. Culotte du Pape. (Pope's Breeches.)

1 ounce of nutmegs.

1/2 do. Ceylon cinnamon.

1/2 do. cloves.

1/4 do. vanilla.

Macerate for 24 hours with 3 1/2 gallons of alcohol, 95 per cent., and 3 1/2 gallons of water: (See No. 5.) Distil from off the water 3 gallons flavored spirit; add 42 lbs. of sugar boiled with 4 1/2 gallons of water. Color pale yellow. (See No. 91.)

143. Curacao d'Hollande. (Holland Curaçoa)

1 lb. of Curaçoa orange peel.

1/4 do. Ceylon cinnamon.

Let them soak in water; boil them for 5 minutes with the juice of 16 oranges and 7 gallons of white plain syrup (see No. 7); then add 3 gallons of alcohol, 95 per cent.; strain, filter; color dark yellow. (See No. 88.)

144. Danziger Drops. (See No. 41.)

2 ounces centaurium.

2 1/2 ounces ginger.

3 do angelica root.

1 1/2 do. nutmegs.

1/2 drachm aloe socotrin.

2 do. Galanga root.

1/2 ounce myrrh.

3/4 do. gentian root.

2 ounces cassia buds.

1 1/2 do. wormwood.

3/4 do. agaric.

Grind and macerate with 4 3/4 gallons of alcohol, 95 per cent., and 5 1/4 gallons. of water (see No. 5); strain, press, filter, and color dark yellow. (See No. 88.)

145. Eau d'Abricots. (Apricot Water.)

80 apricots, very ripe.

Cut in small pieces, and boil them up with 4 gallons of white wine; strain, and add 1 1/4 gallon of white plain syrup (see No. 7); 1/2 an ounce of tincture of cinnamon, and 4¾ gallons of alcohol, 95 per cent.; filter after two weeks.

146. Eau d'Absinthe. (Absinthe Water.)

22 ounces of wormwood.

Macerate 24 hours with 3 gallons of alcohol, 95 per cent., and 3 1/2 gallons of water (see No. 5). Distil from off the water 3 gallons of flavored spirit, and add 8 lbs. of sugar dissolved in 6 1/2 gallons of water; filter, and color green with tincture of saffron and indigo. (See No. 90.)

147. Eau d'Anis. (Water of Anise-seed.)

1 ounce of oil of anise-seed dissolved in 3 gallons of alcohol, 95 per cent.; then add 8 lbs. of sugar dissolved in 6 1/2 gallons of water, and filter. (See No. 3.)

148. Eau d'Anis Compose. (Compound Water of Anise-seed.)

1/2 lb. of green anise-seed,

1/2 lb. of star anise-seed.

1/2 lb. of angelica seed.

Grind; macerate for 24 hours with 3 gallons of alcohol, 95 per cent., and 3 1/2 gallons of water (see No. 5) ; distil from off the water 3 gallons flavored spirit, and add 3 lbs. of sugar dissolved in 6 1/2 gallons of water; then filter. (See No. 3.)

149. Eau Archi-Episcopale.

24 cedrats.

18 ounces of lemon balm.

3 drachms of mace.

6 ounces of angelica root.

2 drachms of reseda flowers.

2 do. jasmin do.

3 quarts of orange-flower water.

Macerate for 24 hours with 3 gallons of alcohol, 95 per cent., and 3 1/2 gallons of water (see No. 5); distil over 3 gallons of flavored spirit, add 8 lbs. of sugar dissolved in 6 1/2 gallons of water. Filter. (See No. 3.)

150. Eau d'Argent. (Silver Water.)

4 drachms of oil of cedrats.

10 drops of oil of roses.

Dissolve in 3 gallons of alcohol, 95 per cent., add 20 lbs. of sugar dissolved in 5 3/4 gallons of water; filter, then add 40 sheets of silverfoil, torn or cut in small pieces.

151. Eau Aromatique. (Aromatic Water.)

13 ounces of Ceylon cinnamon.

5 do. cardamom.

6 1/2 do. sassafras

13 drachms of ginger.

Ground; macerate for 24 hours with 3 gallons of alcohol, 95 per cent., and 3 1/2 gallons of water (see No. 5). Distil over 3 gallons of aromatic spirit; mix with it 8 lbs. of sugar dissolved in 6 1/2 gallons of water. Filter. (See No. 3.)

152. Eau de Belles Dames.

2 3/4 drachms of essence of vanilla.

12 drops of oil of neroly.

8 drops of oil of roses.

Dissolve in 3 gallons of alcohol, 95 per cent.; add 20 lbs. of sugar dissolved in tit gallons of water.

Filter. Color rose. (See No. 93.)

153. Eau de Bergamotte. (Bergamot Water.)

10 oranges, the rinds only.

10 bergamots, do. do.

5 lemons, do. do.

Cut them in small pieces, and macerate for 24 hours with 3 gallons of alcohol, 95 per cent.; add 3 1/2 gallons of water (see No. 5). Distil from off the water 3 gallons of flavored spirit, and add 20 lbs. of sugar, dissolved in 5 3/4 gallons of water. Filter. (See No. 3.)

154. Eau de Cannelle. (Cinnamon Water.)

1 ounce of oil of cinnamon; dissolve in 3 gallons of alcohol, 95 per cent., then add 8 lbs. of sugar dissolved in 6 1/2 gallons of water. Filter. (See No. 3.)

155. Eau de Carvi. (Caraway Water.)

1 1/2 lb. of caraway seed, ground; and macerate for 24 hours with 3 gallons of alcohol, 95 per cent., and 3 1/2 gallons of water (see No. 5). Distil from off the water 3 gallons of flavored spirit, and add 8 lbs. of sugar dissolved in 6 1/2 gallons of water. Filter. (See No. 3.)

156. Eau de Cedrat. (Cedrat Water.)

48 cedrats, the rinds only.

24 oranges, do. do.

Cut and macerate them for 24 hours with 3 gallons of alcohol, 95 per cent., and 3 1/2 gallons of water (see No. 5). Distil from off the water 3 gallons of flavored spirit; add 24 lbs. of sugar dissolved in 5 1/2 gallons of water. Filter. (See No. 3.)

157. Eau de Celery. (Kirschwasser.)

12 ounces celery seed ground. Macerate for 24 hours with 3 gallons of alcohol, 95 per cent., and 3 1/2 gallons of water (see No. 5); distil from off the water the 3 gallons of flavored spirit; then add 24 lbs. of sugar dissolved in 5 1/2 gallons of water. Filter. (See No. 3.)

158. Eau de Cerises. (Cherry Water.)

Take 9 bushels of black cherries, without stems, and make a pulp of them; break two handfuls of cherry stones; put this pulp in a large cask, and let it ferment for 2 or 3 months; keep off the air by a good fixed cover, and add water sufficient to prevent its burning when distilled; then distil over to the strength of 55 per cent. (10 above proof), and fill it in demijohns or bottles.

159. Eau de Chasseurs. (Hunter's Dew.)

145 drops of oil of peppermint.

48 do. oil of mace.

Dissolved in 3 gallons of alcohol, 95 per cent.; then add 8 lbs. of sugar dissolved in 6 1/2 gallons of water. Filter. (See No. 3.)

160. Eau de Cologne, pure. (Cologne Water.)

21 ounces of oil of orange.

21 do. oil of bergamot.

2 5/8 do. oil of neroly.

6 9/16 do. oil of lavender.

3 15/16 do. oil of rosemary.

63 drops of oil of roses.

126 do. oil of cloves.

Dissolve in 10 gallons of alcohol, 95 per cent.

161. Eau de Cologne, a l'Ambregris. (Ambergris Cologne Water.)

21 ounces of oil of orange.

21 do. oil of bergamot.

2 5/8 do. oil of neroly.

6 9/16 do. oil of lavender.

3 15/16 do. oil of rosemary.

63 drops of oil of roses.

126 do. oil of cloves.

200 do. essence of amber.

Dissolve in 10 gallons of alcohol, 95 per cent.

162. Eau de Cologne au Muse. (Musk Cologne Water.)

21 ounces of oil of orange.

21 do. oil of bergamot.

2 5/8 do. oil of neroly.

6 9/16 do. oil of lavender.

3 15/16 do. oil of rosemary.

63 drops of oil of roses.

126 do oil of cloves.

1/2 ounce essence of musk.

Dissolve in 10 gallons of alcohol, 95 per cent.

163. Eau Cordiale. (Cordial Water.)

1 ounce of myrrh.

4 do. cinnamon.

4 do. cardamom.

Ground; macerate for 24 hours with 3 gallons of alcohol, 95 per cent., and 3 1/2 gallons of water (see No. 5); distil over 3 gallons of flavored spirit;

then add 8 lbs. of sugar dissolved in 6 1/2 gallons of water. Filter. (See No. 3.)

164. Eau de Cumin.

1 ounce of oil of caraway seed dissolved in 3 gallons of alcohol, 95 per cent., and then add 8 lbs. of sugar dissolved in 6 1/2 gallons of water. Filter. (See No. 3.)

165. Eau Divine.

1 1/2 lbs. of fresh lemon peel, the yellow only.

1/4 lb. of coriander-seed.

1 ounce of mace.

1 do. cardamom.

Ground; and macerate for 24 hours with 3 gallons of alcohol, 95 per cent. and 3 1/2 gallons of water (see No. 5). Distil from off the water 3 gallons of fine flavored spirit, add 2 drachms of oil of neroly and 1 1/2 drachm of oil of bergamot; after dissolution mix 24 lbs. of sugar dissolved in 5 1/2 gallons of water. Filter. (See No. 3.)

166. Eau de Fleurs d'Oranges.

(Orange-Flower Water.)

162 drops of oil of neroly, dissolve in 3 gallons of alcohol, 95 per cent., then add 8 lbs. of sugar dissolved in 6 1/2 gallons of water. Filter. (See No. 3.)

167. Eau de Fraises. (Strawberry Water.)

6 lbs. of strawberries made to a pulp.

8 lbs. of sugar.

Boil for 5 minutes in 6 1/2 gallons of water; strain, press, then add 3 gallons of alcohol, 95 per cent. Filter. (See No. 3.)

168. Eau de Framboises. (Raspberry Water.)

6 lbs. of raspberries made to a pulp, boil for 5 minutes with 8 lbs. of sugar and 6 1/2 gallons of water; strain, press, and then add 3 gallons of alcohol, 95 per cent. Filter. (See No. 3.)

169. Eau de Génièvre. (Juniper Water.)

3 drachms of oil of juniper, dissolve in 3 gallons of alcohol, 95 per cent., then add 8 lbs. of sugar dissolved in 6 1/2 gallons of water. Filter.

170. Eau de Girofle. (Clove Water.)

10 ounces of cloves.

1 1/4 do. mace.

Ground; macerate for 24 hours with 3 gallons of alcohol, 95 per cent., and 3 1/2 gallons of water (see No. 5). Distil from off the water 3 gallons of flavored spirit, then add 20 lbs. of sugar dissolved in 6 3/4 gallons of water.

Color brown with coloring and filter (see Nos. 3 and 88).

171. Eau de Groseilles. (Currant Water.)

6 lbs. of red currants made to a pulp, boil for 5 minutes with 8 lbs. of sugar and 6 1/2 gallons of water, strain, press. then add 3 gallons of alcohol, 95 per cent. Filter. (See No. 3.)

172. Eau de la Cote, St. Andre.

4 lbs. of peach kernels.

4 ounces of Ceylon cinnamon.

27 oranges, the yellow parts of the rinds of them.

Cut; macerate for 24 hours with 3 gallons of alcohol, 95 percent, and 3 1/2 gallons of water (see No. 5). Distil from off the water 3 gallons of fine flavored spirit, then add 20 lbs. of sugar dissolved in 5 3/4 gallons of water. Filter. (See No. 3.)

173. Eau de Lucrèce.

64 drops of oil of cinnamon.

32 do. oil of cloves.

146 do. oil of cedar.

Dissolve in 3 gallons of alcohol, 95 per cent., then add 20 lbs. of sugar dissolved in 5 3/4 gallons of water. Filter. (See No. 3.)

174. Eau de Malte. (Water of Malta.)

4 ounces of Ceylon cinnamon.

1/2 do. castoreum.

1 do. mace.

Cut and ground; macerate for 24 hours with 3 gallons of alcohol, 95 per cent., and 3 1/2 gallons of water (see No. 5); distil from off the water 3 gallons of flavored spirit; add 20 lbs. of sugar dissolved in 5 3/4 gallons of water. Filter. (See No. 3.)

175. Eau de Menthe. (Mint Water.)

½ ounce of oil of peppermint dissolved in 3 gallons of alcohol, 95 per cent.; then add 8 lbs. of sugar dissolved in 6 1/2 gallons of water. Filter. (See No. 3.)

176. Eau de Mere.

1 lb. of angelica root.

1 lb. of juniper berries.

Ground; macerate for 24 hours with 3 gallons of alcohol, 95 percent., and 6 1/2 gallons of water (see No. 5); strain, press; dissolve in the liquor 8 lbs. of sugar. Filter. (See No. 3.)

177. Eau de Millefleurs. (All-Flower Water.)

12 ounces of orange flowers.

9 do. quincy blossoms.

6 do. lavender flowers.

5 do. orris-root.

5 do. peppermint.

4 do. lemon balm.

4 do. cinnamon.

2 do. thyme.

1 1/2 do. cloves,

Ground; macerate for 24 hours with 3 gallons of alcohol, 95 percent., and 3 1/2 gallons of water (see No. 5); distil from off the water 3 gallons of flavored spirit, and add 20 lbs. of sugar dissolved in 5 3/4 gallons of water; color green with tincture of indigo and saffron, and filter. (See Nos. 3 and 90.)

178. Eau de Noix. (Water of Walnuts.)

54 unripe walnuts pounded to a pulp.

8 ounces of cinnamon.

4 do. cloves.

Ground; macerate for 8 days with 3 gallons of alcohol, 95 per cent. (see No. 5); strain, press, filter; add 8 lbs. of sugar dissolved in 6 1/2 gallons of water; color dark brown. (See No. 88.)

179. Eau de Noyaux de Pfalzburg.

½ lb. of bitter almonds,

½ do. apricot kernels.

¼ do. peach kernels.

½ do. cherry kernels.

Ground; macerate for 24 hours with 3 gallons of alcohol, 95 per cent., and 3 1/2 gallons of water (see No. 5); distil from off the water 3 gallons of fine flavored spirit; mix it with 20 lbs. of sugar dissolved in 5 3/4 gallons of water. Filter. (See No. 3).

180. Eau d'Oillets. (Water of Pinks.)

2 lbs. of red-pink flowers.

1 drachm of cloves.

Ground and cut small; macerate for 24 hours with 3 gallons of alcohol, 95 per cent., and 3 1/2 gallons of water (see No. 5); distil from off the water 3 gallons of fine flavored alcohol; add 20 lbs. of sugar dissolved in 5 3/4 gallons of water; color red. (See No. 93.)

181. Eau d'Or. (Golden Water.)

12 oranges, the yellow rinds only.

12 lemons. do. do. do.

1 1/2 drachms of mace.

3 ounces of cardamom.

3 do. grains d'ambrette.

Ground; macerate for 24 hours with 3 gallons of alcohol, 95 per cent, and 3 3/4 gallons of water (see No. 5). Distil from off the water 3 gallons of flavored spirit, then add 20 lbs. of sugar, dissolved in 5 3/4 gallons of water, filter, mix in 2 sheets of pure gold leaf to each bottle.

182. Eau des Pacificateurs de Grace.

24 lemons, the yellow rinds only; cut and macerate for 24 hours with 3 gallons of alcohol, 95 per cent., and 3 1/2 gallons of water (see No. 5). Distil from off the water 3 gallons of flavored spirit, and add to it 1/2 gallon of orangeflower water and 20 lbs. of sugar dissolved in 5 1/4 gallons of water. Filter. Color red. (See No. 93).

183. Eau de Quatre Graines. (Water of Four Seeds.)

¼ lb. of fennel-seed.

¼ lb. of celery-seed.

1⁄4 lb. of star anise-seed.

1⁄4 lb. of dill-seed.

Ground; macerate for 24 hours with 3 gallons of alcohol, 95 per cent., and 3½ gallons of water (see No. 5). Distil from off the water 3 gallons of fine flavored spirit; then add 20 lbs. of sugar, dissolve in 5 ¾ gallons of water. Filter. (See No. 3).

184. Eau de The. (Tea Water.)

1 lb. of hyson tea.

½ lb. of souchong tea.

Ground; and macerate for 8 days with 3 gallons of alcohol, 95 per cent., and 4 1/2 gallons of water (see No. 5); strain, press and filter; then add 2 1/2 gallons of white plain syrup. (See No. 7.)

185. Eau Verte Stomachique.

3 ounces of coriander-seed.

1 1/2 do. star anise-seed.

3 do. angelica seed.

1½ do. cloves.

3 drachms of Spanish saffron.

6 do. Peruvian balsam.

3 do. mace.

1 1/2 ounce of Ceylon cinnamon.

6 drachms of carrot-seed.

18 accajou nuts.

6 drachms of rosemary.

6 oranges, the yellow rinds only.

6 lemons. do. do. do.

Ground; macerate for 2 weeks with 3 gallons of alcohol, 95 per cent., and 3 1/2 gallons of water (see No. 5). Distil from off the water 3 gallons of high-flavored spirit, mix with 20 lbs. of sugar dissolved in 5 3/4 gallons of water. Filter. Color green (see No. 89.)

186. Eau de Vie d'Andaye.

4 ounces of star anise-seed.

8 do. coriander-seed.

4 do. green anise-seed.

4 do. orris-root.

18 oranges, the yellow rinds only.

Ground and cut; macerate for 24 hours with 3 3/4 gallons of alcohol, 95 per cent., and 4 gallons of water. (See No. 5.) Distil from off the water 3

3/4 gallons of flavored spirit, then add 40 lbs. of sugar dissolved in 3 3/4 gallons of water. Filter. (See No. 3.)

187. Eau de Vie de Danzig.

1 lb. of cacao, roasted.

1/4 do. Ceylon cinnamon.

1/2 do. mace.

13 lemons, the yellow rinds only.

Ground and cut; macerate for 24 hours with 3 3/4 gallons of alcohol, 95 per cent., and 4 gallons of water (see No. 5); distil from off the water 3 ¾ gallons of flavored spirit; mix it with 40 lbs. of sugar dissolved in 3 3/4 gallons of water; filter; color yellow, mixed with gold leaves. (See Nos. 91 and 181.)

188. Eau de Vie de Languedoc.

4 ounces of pearl-barley boiled for 2 hours in 4 gallons of water; add 1 ounce of linden flowers, 1 ounce of alder flowers, 1/2 an ounce of black tea; boil only for 2 minutes; add to this 5 5/8 gallons of alcohol, 95 per cent.; add the following, made into a tincture: 15 grains of crude cassia, 30 grains of Turkey rhubarb, 3/4 of a grain of aloe socotrin, 1/2 an ounce of oak bark; macerate for 48 hours in 3 pints of alcohol (see No. 5); color pale or dark yellow. (See No. 91.)

189. Elixir de Garus.

10 drachms of myrrh.

10 do. aloes.

15 do. cloves.

15 do. nutmegs.

5 ounces of Spanish saffron.

3 1/8 do. Ceylon cinnamon.

Ground and cut; macerate for 8 days with 3 3/4 gallons of alcohol, 95 percent's., and 4 gallons of water, (see No. 5); distil from off the water 3 ¾ gallons of flavored spirit; add 4 1/4 gallons of white plain syrup (see No. 7) and 2 gallons of water; color yellow. (See No. 91.)

190. Elixir de GenievTe. (Elixir of Juniper.)

1 1⁄4 lb. of juniper berries, ground; macerate for 8 days with 3 3⁄4 gallons of alcohol, 95 per cent., and 2 gallons of water; press, strain, and filter; add 4 1/4 gallons of white plain syrup. (See No. 7.)

191. Elixir of Long Life.

2 ounces of Zedoary root.

2 do. agaric.

2 do. gentian root.

2 do. Venetian theriak.

2 do. Turkey rhubarb.

2 do. angelica root.

4 do. ginger.

Ground; macerate for 2 weeks with 4 3⁄4 gallons of alcohol, 95 per cent. (see No. 5); then add 5 1/4 gallons of water. Filter. (See No. 3.)

192. Elixir de Neroly.

2 ounces of myrrh, ground; macerate for 8 days in 3 3⁄4 gallons of alcohol, 95 per cent.; add 97 drops of oil of neroly; mix it with 20 lbs. of sugar dissolved in 5 gallons of water. Filter. (See No. 3.)

193. Elixir des Troubadours.

4 lbs. of musk roses.

1 1/2 do. jasmin flowers.

1 lb. of orange flowers.

1/2 ounce of mace.

2 do. Ravenzara nuts, or allspice.

Cut, and macerate for 2 weeks with 3 3⁄4 gallons of alcohol, 95 per cent., and 4 gallons of water (see No. 5); distil from off the water 3 ¾ gallons of alcohol well flavored; add 20 lbs. of sugar dissolved in 5 gallons of water; filter; color rose. (See No. 93.)

194. Elixir de Violettes.

3 gallons of syrup of violets.

2 do. syrup of raspberries (see No. 356).

5 do. spirit, 60 per cent.

Mix and filter.

195. Escubac d'Irelande.

12 ounces of Italian fennel-seed.

8 do. Ceylon cinnamon.

Ground; macerate for 24 hours with 3 1⁄3 gallons of alcohol, 95 per cent., and 4 gallons of water (see No. 5); distil from off the water 3 1⁄3 gallons of flavored spirit; add 6 2⁄3 gallons of white plain syrup, filter, and color yellow. (See Nos. 3, 7, and 91.)

196. Esprit de Manuel.

100 drops of oil of peppermint.

59 do. oil of cloves.

Dissolve in 3 1⁄3 gallons of alcohol, 95 per cent.; add 6 2⁄3 gallons of white plain syrup; color green with saffron and indigo. (See Nos. 7 and 90.)

197. Essence of Ginger.

2 lbs. of ground ginger.

6 gallons of alcohol, 95 per cent.

4 do. of water.

Macerate for 2 weeks (see No. 5), strain, and filter.

198. Essence of Lemon.

2 ounces of oil of lemon dissolved in 6 gallons of alcohol, 95 per cent.; add 4 gallons of water; filter; color yellow. (See No. 91.)

199. Essence of Peppermint.

2 ounces of oil of peppermint dissolved in 6 gallons of alcohol, 95 per cent.; add 4 gallons of water; color with tincture of turmeric. Filter. (See No. 91.) 200. Essence of "Wintergreen. 2 ounces of oil of wintergreen dissolved in 6 gallons of alcohol, 95 per cent.; add 4 gallons of water; color red with tincture of sanders wood; filter. (See No. 3.)

201. Extrait d'Absinthe.

26 2/3 ounces of Italian fennel-seed.

5 lbs. of green anise-seed.

13 2/3 ounces of liquorice-root.

3 2/3 drachms of calamus-root.

Ground; macerate for 24 hours with 7 3/4 gallons of alcohol, 95 per cent., and 6 1/4 gallons of water (see No. 5); distil over till running 45 per cent.; macerate the distilled liquor for 48 hours with 4 1/2 ounces of peppermint and 12 ounces of Pontic wormwood; press and filter.

202. Fining with Milk.

¾ of a pint of good milk, boiled and cooled again, mixed with 10 gallons of liquor; it will soon settle it.

203. Fining with Eggs.

2 egg whites beaten to froth; add a little alcohol; mix it with 10 gallons of liquor; it will soon settle it.

204. Fining with Potash.

1 1/2 ounce of carbonate of potash, dissolved in 1 pint of water, mixed with 10 gallons of liquor, will soon settle it.

205. Fining with Alum.

3 drachms of powdered calcinated alum dissolved in alcohol, and mixed with 10 gallons of liquor, will soon settle it.

206. Fever Drops.

5 1/4 lbs. of calamus-root.

1 3/4 do. zedoary.

1 3/4 do. ginger.

3 1/2 do. dried orange apples.

Ground; macerate for 8 days in 5 gallons of alcohol, 80 per cent. (see No. 5); strain, press, and filter; then add 4 to 6 ounces of alcoholic extract of Peruvian bark dissolved in 5 gallons of alcohol, 80 per cent. Filter. (See No. 3.)

Dose 3 to 4 teaspoonfuls a day.

207. Gerofline.

½ ounce of oil of cloves dissolved in 3 gallons of alcohol, 95 per cent.; add 2 1/2 gallons of white plain syrup (see No. 7), and 4 1/2, gallons of water. Filter. Color yellow.

208. Gin, Domestic.

3 drachms of oil of juniper; dissolve in 5 1/4 gallons of alcohol, 95 per cent.; add 4 5/8 gallons of water and ⅛ gallon of white plain syrup. (See No. 7.)

209. Gin, English.

3 drachms of oil of juniper.

1 drachm of oil of turpentine.

Dissolve in 5 1/4 gallons of alcohol, 95 per cent.; add 4 3/4 gallons of water.

210. Gin, Holland.

2 1/2 gallons of Holland gin.

3 ¾ do. alcohol, 95 per cent. .

3 3/4 do. water, mixed together.

211. Gin, London Cordial.

3 drachms of oil of juniper.

1 do. oil of angelica.

10 drops of oil of coriander.

Dissolve in 5 1/4 gallons of alcohol, 95 per cent.; add 1/2 gallon of white plain syrup (see No. 7), and 4 1⁄4 gallons of water. Filter.

212. Ginger Beer.

10 gallons of boiling water.

10 ounces of cream of tartar.

15 do. ground ginger.

10 lemons cut in slices and boiled together; let them stand until nearly cool; strain and press them. Dissolve in this mixture 15 lbs. of sugar, and add when lukewarm, one pint of yeast; let the compound stand for 14 hours skim and filter ; bottle and bind the corks.

213. Hop Beer.

2 ounces of hops boiled for 10 minutes in 10 gallons of water, with 16 lbs. of sugar; then skim and strain; let it cool to 80 degrees, Fahrenheit; add 1 1/2 pint of brewers' yeast, and let it stand for 24 hours; filter, and fill it in an iron-bound and well pitched cask, and bung it up tight.

214. Huile d' Absinthe, (Oil of Absinthe.)

1 1⁄2 lb. of wormwood.

1 lb. of green anise-seed.

1 lb. of fennel-seed.

Ground; macerate for 10 days in 4 gallons of alcohol, 95 per cent.; add 5 gallons of water (see No. 5). Distil from off the water 4 gallons of flavored spirit; mix it with 48 lbs. of sugar, boiled for 3 hours with 3 gallons of water, filling up as it evaporates; skim, mix, filter, while warm. Sweet-oil color.

215. Huile d'Amour. (Oil of Love.)

8 ounces of moldavique seed.

4 do. sprouts of rosemary with flowers.

16 do. lemon balm.

Ground; macerate for 10 days in 4 gallons of alcohol, 95 per cent.; add 5 gallons of water (see No. 5). Distil from off the water 4 gallons of flavored spirit, and mix it with 48 lbs. of sugar boiled for 3 hours with 3 gallons of water, filling up as it evaporates; skim, mix, filter while warm. Color green. (See No. 90.)

216. Huile d'Ananas. (Pineapple Oil.)

4 lbs. of pineapples, grated; macerate them with 4 gallons of alcohol, 95 per cent., for one week (see No. 5). Strain, press and filter; add a syrup made of 48 lbs. of sugar boiled for 3 hours with 3 gallons of water, filling up as it evaporates; skim, mix, filter if necessary. (See No. 7.)

217. Huile d'Angelique. (Oil of Angelica.)

12 ounces of angelica-root.

2 do. Ceylon cinnamon.

Ground ; macerate for 10 days in 4 gallons of alcohol, 95 per cent., and 5 gallons of water (see No. 5). Distil from off the water 4 gallons of flavored spirit; mix it with 48 lbs. of sugar boiled for 3 hours with 3 gallons of water, filling up as it evaporates; skim, mix and filter warm. (See No. 7.)

218. Huile d'Anis. (Oil of Anise-seed.)

3 drachms of oil of anise-seed.

1/2 ounce of tincture of vanilla.

Dissolve in 4 gallons of alcohol, 95 per cent.; add a syrup made of 48 lbs. of sugar boiled for 3 hours with 3 gallons of water, filling up as it evaporates; skim, mix, filter warm if necessary. (See No. 7.)

219. Huile de Bergamot. (Oil of Bergamot.)

1/2 ounce of oil of bergamot.

1 drachm of oil of orange.

Dissolve in 4 gallons of alcohol, 95 per cent.; add a syrup made of 48 lbs. of sugar boiled for 3 hours with 3 gallons of water, filling up as it evaporates (See No. 7); skim, mix, filter warm if necessary.

220. Huile de Cannelle. (Cinnamon Oil.)

1/2 ounce of oil of cinnamon, dissolved in 4 gallons of alcohol, 95 per cent.; add a syrup made of 48 lbs. of sugar boiled for 3 hours with 3 gallons of water, filling up as it evaporates; skim, mix, filter warm if necessary. (See No. 7.)

221. Huile de Celery. (Celery on.)

3/4 lb. of celery seed, ground; macerate for 10 days with 4 gallons of alcohol, 95 per cent., and 5 gallons of water. (See No. 5.) Distil from off the water 4 gallons of flavored spirit; add a syrup made of 48 lbs. of sugar boiled for three hours with 3 gallons of water, filling up as it evaporates; skim, mix, filter warm if necessary. (See No. 7.)

222. Huile des Chasseurs. (Hunter's Oil.)

20 drops of oil of mace.

12 do. oil of spearmint.

8 do. oil of neroly.

120 do. oil of peppermint.

Dissolve in 4 gallons of alcohol, 95 per cent.; add a syrup made of 48 lbs. of sugar boiled for 3 hours with 3 gallons of water, filling up as it evaporates; skim, mix, filter warm. Color green. (See Nos. 7 and 90.)

223. Huile de Citron. (Lemon Oil.)

½ ounce of oil of lemon, dissolved in 4 gallons of alcohol, 95 per cent.; add a syrup made of 48 lbs. of sugar boiled for 3 hours with 3 gallons of water, filling up as it evaporates; skim, mix, filter warm. Color yellow. (See Nos. 7 and 91.)

224. Huile de Fleurs d'Orange. (Oil of Orange Flowers.)

50 drops of oil of neroly dissolved in 4 gallons of alcohol, 95 per cent.; add a syrup made of 48 lbs. of sugar boiled for 3 hours with 3 gallons of water, filling up as it evaporates; skim, mix, filter warm. (See No. 7.)

225. Huile de Gerofle. (Oil of Cloves.)

3 drachms of oil of cloves dissolved in 4 gallons of alcohol, 95 per cent.; add a syrup made of 48 lbs. of sugar boiled for 3 hours with 3 gallons of water, filling up as it evaporates; skim, mix, filter warm; color dark yellow. (See Nos. 7 and 91.)

226. Huile de Jasmin. (Oil of Jasmin.)

4 lbs. of jasmin flowers.

Macerate them for 2 weeks with 4 gallons of alcohol, 95 per cent. (see No. 5); strain and press; add a syrup made of 48 lbs. of sugar boiled for 3 hours with 3 gallons 0f water, filling up as it evaporates, skim, mix, filter warm, (See No. 7.)

227. Huile de Jupiter. (Oil of Jove.)

8 ounces of Italian fennel-seed.

8 do. cinnamon.

8 do. roasted cacao.

4 do. orris-root.

Ground; macerate for 10 days with 4 gallons of alcohol, 95 per cent., and 5 gallons of water (see No. 5); distil from off the water 4 gallons of flavored spirit; add a syrup made of 48 lbs. of sugar boiled for 3 hours with 3 gallons of water, filling up as it evaporates; skim, mix, filter warm. (See No. 7.)

228. Huile de Kirschwasser. (Oil of Kirschwasser.)

4 gallons of Kirschwasser; add a syrup made of 48 lbs. of sugar boiled for 3 hours with 3 gallons of water, filling up as it evaporates; skim, mix, filter warm. (See No. 7.)

229. Huile de Menthe. (Oil of Mint.)

1/2 an ounce of oil of peppermint dissolved in 4 gallons of alcohol, 95 per cent.; add a syrup made of 48 lbs. of sugar boiled for 3 hours with 3 gallons of water, filling up as it evaporates; skim, mix, filter warm. (See No. 7.)

230. Huile de Muscade. (Oil of Mace.)

½ an ounce of oil of mace dissolved in 4 gallons of alcohol, 95 per cent.; add a syrup made of 48 lbs. of sugar boiled for 3 hours with 3 gallons of water, filling up as it evaporates; skim, mix, filter warm. (See No. 7.)

231. Huile de Myrrhe. (Oil of Myrrh.)

2 ounces of myrrh.

4 do. cinnamon.

Ground; macerate for 10 days with 4 gallons of alcohol, 95 per cent. (see No. 5); strain, press; then add a syrup made of 48 lbs. of sugar boiled for 3 hours with 3 gallons of water, filling up as it evaporates; skim, mix, filter, warm. (See No. 7.)

232. Huile de Sept Grains. (Oil of Seven Seeds.)

6 ounces of green anise-seed.

3 do. dill-seed.

3 do. coriander-seed.

3 do. fennel-seed.

3 do. star anise-seed.

3 do. caraway-seed.

1 1/2 do. celery-seed.

Ground; macerate for 10 days with 4 gallons of alcohol, 95 per cent., and 5 gallons of water (see No. 5); distil from off the water 4 gallons of flavored spirit; add a syrup made of 48 lbs. of sugar boiled for 3 hours in 3 gallons of water, filling up as it evaporates; skim, mix, filter warm. (See No. 7.)

233. Huile de Rose. (Oil of Roses.)

50 drops of oil of roses dissolved in 4 gallons of alcohol, 95 per cent.; add a syrup made of 48 lbs. of sugar boiled for 3 hours in 3 gallons of water; fill up as it evaporates; skim, mix, filter warm; color rose. (See Nos. 7 and 93.)

234. Huile Royale. (Royal Oil.)

4 ounces of ground cloves.

4 do. cinnamon.

4 do. myrrh.

8 do. carrot-seed.

10 oranges, the yellow rinds only.

Macerate for 10 days with 4 gallons of alcohol, 95 per cent., and 5 gallons of water (see No. 5); distil from off the water 4 gallons of flavored spirit; add a syrup made of 48 lbs. of sugar boiled for 3 hours with 3 gallons of water; fill up as it evaporates; skim, mix, filter warm. (See No. 7.)

235. Huile de Rhum.

2 3/4 ounces of maidenhair.

2 3/4 do. Ceylon cinnamon.

Ground and cut; add to the following syrup when nearly done: take 48 lbs. of sugar, boil it for 3 hours' with 3 gallons of water, filling up as it evaporates (see No. 7); skim, press, and filter; then add 4 gallons of good Jamaica rum.

236. Huile de Thé. (Oil of Tea.)

48 lbs. of sugar to be boiled for 3 hours with 3 gallons of water; fill up as it evaporates (see No. 7); add 8 ounces of imperial tea; strain, press; add 4 gallons of alcohol, 95 per cent.; filter warm.

237. Huile de Vanille. (Vanilla Oil.)

2 drachms of vanilla, cut and rubbed, with 1 ounce of sugar; add 13 drops of oil of roses; dissolve in 4 gallons of alcohol, 95 per cent.; then add a syrup made of 48 lbs. of sugar boiled for 3 hours in 3 gallons of water, filling up as it evaporates (see No. 7); skim, mix, and filter warm.

238. Huile de Venus. (Oil of Venus)

5 ounces of carrot flowers.

5 do. green anise-seed.

5 ounces of caraway-seed

15 oranges, only the yellow rind.

Cut and ground; macerate for 10 days with 4 gallons of alcohol, 95 per cent., and 5 gallons of water (see No. 5); distil from off the water 4 gallons of flavored spirit; then add a syrup made of 48 lbs. of sugar boiled for 3 hours with 3 gallons of water, filling up as it evaporates (see No. 7); skim, mix, and filter warm.

239. Huile de Violettes. (Violet on.)

48 lbs. of sugar boiled for 3 hours with 3 gallons of water, filling up as it evaporates (see No. 7); skim; take from the fire, and add 8 ounces of violet flowers; let it nearly cool, and then add 4 gallons of alcohol, 95 per cent.; strain and filter; color violet with tincture of indigo and cochineal. (See No. 94.)

240. Hydromel Vineux (Metheglin). (Wine Mead.)

16 lbs. of honey, dissolved in 9 gallons of water, heated to 84 degrees of Fahrenheit; add pint of good brewers' yeast, mix this well and put it in a clean 10-gallon keg, fill it to the bung and put it in a warm place; during fermention keep the keg full with the balance of the liquor. When the fermentation is over keep it well bunged in a cool place.

241. Hypocras à l'Angelique. (Angelica Hippocras.)

10 ounces of angelica-root.

1 ounce of nutmegs.

Ground; macerate for 2 days with 9 gallons of claret wine (see No. 5); then add 8 lbs. of sugar in powder, and 1/2 gallon of alcohol, 95 per cent. Filter. (See No. 3.)

242. Hypocras au Cedrat. (Cedrat Hippocras.)

40 cedrats, the rinds of them cut; add 1/2 gallon of alcohol, 95 per cent., and 9 gallons of good claret wine; macerate for 2 days (see No. 5); add 8 lbs. of sugar in powder; when dissolved. Filter. (See No. 3.)

243. Hypocras Framboisé. (Raspberry Hippocras.)

3 lbs. of raspberries made to a pulp; add 9 gallons of claret wine, and gallon of alcohol, 95 per cent. Dissolve 8 lbs. of sugar in powder in it. Filter. (See No. 3.)

244. Hypocras au Génièvre. (Juniper Hippocras.)

2 1/2 lbs. of ground juniper berries; macerate for 2 days with 9 gallons of claret wine, and gallon of alcohol, 95 per cent. (See No. 5.) Dissolve and add 8 lbs. of powdered sugar; strain and filter.

245. Hypocras aux Noyaux. (Noyau Hippocras.)

480 apricot stones.

240 peach do.

Broken without touching the kernels; macerate stones and kernels together for 2 days with 9 gallons of White French wine, and gallon of alcohol, 95 per cent. (see No. 5); dissolve it in 8 lbs. of powdered sugar. Strain and filter. (See No. 3.)

246. Hypocras Simple.

5 ounces of cinnamon.

2 drachms of cloves.

1 do. Mace.

Ground; macerate for 2 days with ½ gallon of alcohol, 95 per cent. (see No. 5); add one drachm of essence of amber, and dissolve 8 lbs. of powdered sugar in 9 gallons of claret wine; strain and filter. (See No. 3.)

247. Hypocras à la Vanille. (Vanilla Hippocras.)

1 ounce of vanilla powdered with 8 lbs. of sugar. Dissolve them in 9 gallons of claret wine; add 1/2 gallon of alcohol, 95 per cent. Filter.

248. Hypocras au Vin d'Absinthe. (Absinthe Hippoeras)

2 ½ lbs. of fresh wormwood; macerate for 12 hours in 9 gallons of white wine (see No. 5), filter; add to this

40 lemons, the thin yellow rinds only.

40 cedrats. do. do. do. do.

5 ounces of anise-seed.

½ do. cloves.

Ground and cut; macerate the whole with gallon of alcohol, 95 per cent.; add 8 lbs. of powdered sugar; strain and filter. (See No. 5.)

249. Hypocras à laViolette. (Violet Hippocras.)

7 1/2 ounces of orris-root.

1 do. cloves.

Ground; macerate for 2 days with 9 gallons of claret wine and 1/2 gallon of alcohol, 95 per cent. (see No. 5). Dissolve in it 8 lbs. of powdered sugar ; strain, filter; add 40 drops of essence of amber, and 40 drops of essence of musk.

250. Imperial Nectar.

8 lemons, the yellow rinds only.

10 oranges. do. do. do.

6 ounces of Ceylon cinnamon.

½ do. mace.

8 do. star anise-seed.

8 do. coriander-seed.

4 do. juniper berries.

2 do. angelica-seed.

2 drachms of Spanish saffron.

Ground and cut; macerate for 10 days with 4 gallons of alcohol, 95 per cent., and 5 gallons of water (see No. 5). Distil from off the water 4 gallons of flavored alcohol, and add a syrup made of 20 lbs. of sugar boiled with 4 1/2 gallons of water; when nearly cold mix in 1/2 gallon of rose-water. Filter, and color rose. (See No. 93.)

251. Instantaneous Beer.

9 1/2 gallons of water.

1/4 do. lemon-juice,

1 1/2 ounce of ginger powder.

10 lbs of sugar. Dissolve and mix together; continue stirring while bottling (strong bottles) get corks, mallet and string at hand, then add, for each bottle separate, one drachm of bicarbonate of soda; cork and string it quick.

252. Lait de Vieillesse. (Milk of Old Age.)

1 drachm of tincture of Peruvian balsam mixed with 3 gallons of alcohol, 95 per cent.; then add 20 lbs. of sugar, dissolved in 5 1/2 gallons of water; mix in gallon of orangeflower water. Filter. (See No. 93.)

253. Lait Virginale. (Virgin's Milk.)

1/2 ounce of oil of lemon, disolve in 3 gallons of alcohol, 95 per cent.; add 20 lbs. of sugar dissolved in 5 1/3 gallons of water; mix with it gallon of vinegar and gallon of lemon-juice. Filter.

254. Lait de Vecchia. (Milk of Veechia.)

1 1/2 lb. of roasted cacao.

1/4 lb. of cinnamon.

1/4 lb. of carrot-seed.

Ground; macerate for 24 hours with 3 gallons of alcohol, 95 per cent, and 3 1⁄2 gallons of water (see No. 5). Distil from off the water 3 gallons of flavored spirit, then add 20 lbs. of sugar dissolved in 5 3⁄4 gallons of water. Filter. (See No. 3.)

255. Lemonade Effervescing.

10 ounces of powdered tartaric acid.

4 lbs. 6 oz., do. sugar.

1 drachm of oil of lemon mixed together;

keep it dry; mark it No. 1.

10 ounces of bicarbonate of soda.

4 lbs. 6 oz. of powdered sugar.

1 drachm of oil of lemon mixed together; keep dry; mark it No. 2.

Direction: 1⁄2 ounce of No. 1 in one tumbler of water; dissolve ½ ounce of No. 2, put in another tumbler mixed, gives a splendid lemonade.

256. Lemonade for Bottling.

10 ounces of citric acid.

15 lbs. of sugar.

160 drops of oil of lemon.

Rub the sugar with the oil of lemon ; mix in the powdered citric acid, dissolve the whole in 9 gallons of water, filter and fill it in soda-water bottles; add to each bottle drachm of bicarbonate of soda in pieces; cork and string.

257. Lemonade, Plain, in Powder.

(For Ten Gallons.)

½ lb. of tartaric acid in powder.

16 lbs. of sugar in powder.

1 1⁄2 drachm of oil of lemons.

Rub and mix it well. 1 ounce of this powder makes ½ a pint of lemonade.

258. Life of Man.

2 drachms of oil of lemons.

1 1⁄2 do. oil of cloves.

27 drops of oil of mace.

Dissolve in 3 gallons of alcohol, 95 per cent.; then add 24 lbs. of sugar dissolved in 5 ½ gallons of water; filter; color dark rose.(See No. 93.)

259. Liqueur a la Cambron.

64 grains of vanilla.

4 ounces of cinnamon.

4 do. orris-root.

Ground; macerate for 24 hours with 3 gallons of alcohol, 95 per cent, and 3 1⁄2 gallons of water (see No. 5); distil from off the water 3 gallons of flavored spirit; add 24 lbs. of sugar dissolved in 5 1⁄2 gallons of water; filter; color red. (See No. 93.)

260. Liqueur des Amis Reunis.

8 ounces of orris-root.

1 do. of myrrh.

4 ounces of cinnamon.

64 grains of vanilla.

Ground; macerate for 24 hours with 3 gallons of alcohol, 95 per cent. (see No. 5), and 3 1⁄2 gallons of water; distil from off the water 3 gallons of flavored spirit; mix with 24 lbs. of sugar dissolved in 5 1⁄2 gallons of water; filter. (See No. 3.)

261. Liqueur des Braves. (Spirit of Mars)

4 ounces of carrot-seed.

4 do. cardamom-seed.

8 do. roasted cacao.

4 do. Ceylon cinnamon.

Ground; macerate for 24 hours with 3 gallons of alcohol, 95 per cent., and 3 1⁄2 gallons of water (see No. 5); distil from off the water 3 gallons of flavored spirit; add 24 lbs. of sugar dissolved in 5 1⁄2 gallons of water; filter. (See No. 3.)

262. Liqueur de Cafe. (Spirit of Coffee.)

3 lbs. of light-brown roasted coffee ground and boiled for 2 minutes with 2 gallons of water; strain, when cool; add 24 lbs. of sugar dissolved in 3 1/2 gallons of water; add 3 gallons of alcohol, 95 per cent.; filter. (See No. 3.)

263. Liqueur de Cannelle. (Spirit of Cinnamon.)

2 lbs. of cinnamon, ground; macerate for 24 hours with 3 gallons of alcohol, 95 per cent., and 3 1⁄2 gallons of water (see No. 5); distil from off the water 3 gallons of flavored spirit; add 24 lbs. of sugar dissolved in 5 1⁄2 gallons of water; filter; colr red. (See No. 93.)

264. Liqueur de Citron. (Spirit of Lemon.)

3 lbs. of lemon rinds, only the yellow part.
Cut and macerate for 24 hours with 3 gallons of alcohol, 95 per cent., and 3 1/3 gallons of water (see No. 5); distil from off the water 3 gallons of flavored spirit; add 24 lbs. of sugar dissolved in 5 gallons of water; filter; color yellow. (See No. 91.)

265. Liqueur de Fleurs d'Oranges.

(Spirit of Orange Flowers.)
1 gallon of orange-flower water added to a syrup made of 24 lbs. of sugar dissolved in 4 1⁄2, gallons of water; mix with 3 gallons of alcohol, 95 per cent.; filter. (See No. 7.)

266. Liqueur de Fraises. (Spirit of Strawberries.)

10 lbs. of strawberries, boiled for 5 minutes with a syrup made of 24 lbs. of sugar, dissolved in 5 1⁄2 gallons of water; strain, and add 3 gallons of alcohol, 95 per cent.; filter. (See Nos. 3 and 7.)

267. Liqueur de Framboises. (Spirit of Raspberries.)

10 lbs. of raspberries, boiled for 5 minutes with a syrup made of 24 lbs. of sugar, dissolved in 5 1/2 gallons of water. Strain, and add 3 gallons of alcohol, 95 per cent.; filter. (See Nos. 3 and 7.)

268. Liqueur de Groseilles. (Spirit of Currants.)

10 lbs. of red currants, boiled for 5 minutes with a syrup made of 24 lbs. of sugar, dissolved in gallons of water. Strain, and add 3 gallons of alcohol, 95 per cent.; filter. (See Nos. 3 and 7.)

269. Liqueur de Mellisse. (Spirit of Lemon Balm.)

½ an ounce of oil of lemon balm, dissolved in 3 gallons of alcohol, 95 per cent.; add 24 lbs. of sugar, dissolved in 5 1/2 gallons of water; filter. Color deep green, with tincture of indigo and saffron. (See No. 90.)

270. Liqueur d'Orange. (Spirit of Oranges.)

2 lbs. of Curaçoa orange peels, ground; macerate for 24 hours with 3 gallons of alcohol, 95 per cent., and 3 1/2 gallons of water (see No. 5); distil from off the water 3 gallons of flavored spirit, add 24 lbs. of sugar, dissolved in 4 3/4 gallons of water, mix with it 1 gallon of orange-flower water; filter. Color green, with tincture of saffron and indigo. (See No. 90.)

271. Liqueur d'Orgeat. (Spirit of Orgeat.)

3 lbs. of sweet almonds.

1 lb. of bitter almonds.

1 gallon of boiling water; let them stand together till nearly cold; take the skins off by pressing with the fingers; grind, and macerate for 10 days, with 3 gallons of alcohol, 95 per cent, (see No. 5); strain and press; add ½ gallon of orange-flower water and 24 lbs. of sugar, dissolved in 5 gallons of water; filter. (See No. 3.)

272. Liqueur de Roses. (Spirit of Roses.)

5 lbs. of rose leaves.

3 ounces of cinnamon.

1 do. fennel-seed.

The two latter ground; macerate for 24 hours with 3 gallons of alcohol, 95 per cent., and 4 gallons of water (see No. 5). Distil over 3 gallons of flavored spirit; add 24 lbs. of sugar dissolved in 5 1/2 gallons of water; filter. Color rose. (See No. 93.)

273. Liqueur Stomachique.

6 ounces of orange peels.

4 do. lemon.

2 do. anise-seed.

1 1/2 do. galanga-root.

1 1/2 do. cinnamon.

1 1/2 do. orris-root.

1 1/2 do. basil.

1 1/2 do. large camomile flowers.

1 do. lavender flowers.

1 do. rosemary.

½ do. vanilla.

½ do. nutmeg.

½ do. mace.

½ do. cubebs.

½ do. cardamom.

Ground; macerate for 24 hours with 3 gallons of alcohol, 95 per cent.; and 4 gallons of water (see No. 5); distil from off the water 3 gallons of flavored alcohol, add 24 lbs. of sugar, dissolved in 5 1/2 gallons of water; color red-yellow, with a tincture of saffron and cochineal. Filter. (See Nos. 91 and 93.)

274. Liqueur de Thé. (Spirit of Tea.)

24 lbs. of sugar and 5 1/2 gallons of water; boil and skim, then add 8 ounces of the best Hyson tea; let it stand till nearly cool, strain, press; mix

with it 3 gallons of alcohol, 95 per cent. Filter. (One ounce of tincture of Spanish saffron may do well.)

275. Lovage.

8 gallons of Holland gin are mixed with one gallon of syrup, a tincture made of 4 lbs. of finely cut celery roots; macerate for 24 hours with one gallon of alcohol, 95 per cent. (see No. 5); strain, and press the alcohol very well out, and dissolve 6 drachms of oil of cinnamon and 2 drachms of oil of caraway-seed; filter. (See No. 3.)

276. Macaroni.

4 lbs of bitter almonds.

8 ounces of cinnamon.

8 do. nutmegs.

Ground; macerate for 24 hours with 3 gallons of alcohol, 95 per cent., and 3 1/2 gallons of water (see No. 5). Distil from off the water 3 gallons of flavored spirit, and add 24 lbs. of sugar, dissolved in 3 ½ gallons of water. Filter. (See No. 3.)

277. Marasquin de Coings.

48 quinces grated.

1 ounce of peach kernels broken.

Macerate for 24 hours in 3 1/2 gallons of alcohol, 95 per cent., and 3 1/2 gallons of water. Distil over 3 gallons of flavored alcohol, and add 7 gallons of the whitest plain syrup. (See No. 7.)

278. Marasquin de Fraises.

10 lbs. of strawberries made to a pulp; macerate for 24 hours with 3 1/2 gallons of alcohol, 95 per cent., and 3 1/2 gallons of water (see No. 5). Distil from off the water 3 gallons of flavored alcohol, and add 2 gallons of the whitest plain syrup. (See No. 7.)

279. Marasquin de Framboises.

10 lbs. of raspberries made to a pulp; macerate for 24 hours with 3 1/2 gallons of alcohol, 95 per cent., and 3 ½ gallons of water (see No. 5). Distil from off the water 3 gallons of flavored alcohol, and add 7 gallons of the whitest plain syrup. (See No. 7.)

280. Marasquin de Groseilles.

10 lbs. of red currants made to a pulp; macerate for 24 hours with 3 1/2 gallons of alcohol, 95 per cent. and 3 1/2 gallons of water (see No. 5); distil from off the water 3 gallons of flavored alcohol, and add 2 gallons of the whitest plain syrup. (See No. 7.)

281. Marasquin de Peches.

12 lbs. of peaches made to a pulp; only a few stones broken; macerate for 24 hours with 3 1/2 gallons of alcohol, 95 per cent., and gallons of water (see No. 5). Distil from off the water 3 gallons of flavored alcohol, and add 2 gallons of the whitest plain syrup. (See No. 7.)

282. Marasquino di Zara.

9 lbs. of raspberries.

6 lbs. of sour red cherries.

3 lbs. of orange flowers.

Made to a pulp with stones; macerate for 24 hours with 3 1/2 gallons of alcohol, 95 per cent., and 3 1/2 gallops of water (see No. 5). Distil from off the water 3 gallons of flavored alcohol, and add 7 gallons of the whitest plain syrup. (See No. 7.)

283. Mirabolanti, Italian.

1 lb. of ground mirabolanti.

½ do. cardamom.

Macerate for 24 hours with 3 gallons of alcohol, 95 per cent., and 3 gallons of water (see No. 5); distil from off the water 3 gallons of flavored spirit, and add 24 lbs. of sugar dissolved in gallons of water; filter. (See No. 3.)

284. Nectar des Dieux. (Nectar of Olympus.)

2 lbs. of honey.

1 do. coriander-seed.

½ do. fresh lemon peel.

2 ounces of cloves.

4 do. styrax calamita.

4 do. benzoin.

Ground and cut; macerate for 2 weeks with 3 1/2 gallons of alcohol, 95 per cent., and 3 1/2 gallons of water (see No. 5); distil from off the water 3 gallons of flavored spirit, and add 8 ounces of orange water, 1 1/2 drachm of tincture of vanilla, and 30 lbs. of sugar dissolved in 5 1/8 gallons of water; filter; color deep red. (See No. 93.)

285. Nordhaeuser Korn Branntwein.

45 drops of oil of star anise-seed.

6 ⅔ drachms of acetic ether.

7 ounces of St. John's bread (Johannisbrod).

½ drachm of Spanish saffron.

1 do. gunpowder tea.

6 drachms of cinnamon.

Cut, macerate, and dissolve for 24 hours with 5 gallons of the purest alcohol, 95 per cent, (see No. 5); then add 22 1/2 grains tartaric acid dissolved in 5 gallons of water; color yellow; filter. (See Nos. 3 and 91.)

286. Oglio di Venere. (Oil of Venus.)

1 1/2 lb. of cardamom.

¼ do. graines d'ambrettes.

1/4 do. cinnamon.

1/2 do. myrrh.

16 oranges, the yellow rinds of.

Ground; macerate for 24 hours with 3 gallons of alcohol, 95 per cent., and 3 1/2 gallons of water (see No. 5); distil from off the water 3 gallons of flavored alcohol; add 24 lbs. of sugar dissolved in 5 1/2 gallons of water; sweet oil color; filter. (See No. 3.)

287. Orange Nectar.

1 ounce of oil of neroly.

40 oranges, only the yellow rinds.

Macerate for 8 days in 3 gallons of alcohol, 95 per cent. (see No. 5); add 24 lbs. of sugar dissolved in 5 1⁄2 gallons of water; filter; color yellow. (See No. 91.)

288. Orangeade.

40 oranges, the rinds only, powdered with

10 lbs. of sugar.

8 gallons of water.

Dissolved and mixed together in a boiler or tub.

80 oranges, the juice only.

40 lemons, the juice only.

Mix together, and add to the first mixture; filter.

289. Parfait Amour. (Perfect Love.)

8 ounces of cedrat rinds.

4 do. lemon peels.

½ do. cloves.

Ground; macerate for 24 hours with 3 gallons of alcohol, 95 per cent., and 3 1/2 gallons of water (see No. 5); distil from off the water 3 gallons of flavored alcohol; add 30 lbs. of sugar dissolved in 5 1/8 gallons of water; color deep red, and filter. (See Nos. 3 and 93.)

290. Porter,

2 1/2 gallons of brown malt.

3 3/4 ounces of hops.

2 1⁄2 do. molasses.

3 3/4 do. liquorice.

6 grains of pimentum.

24 do. extract of Spanish liquorice.

7 1/2 do. coculi indici.

22 1/2 do. ginger.

3 do. heading, or extract of dark burned malt.

½ pint of coloring (see No. 88.)

½ do. half-burnt coloring.

All substantial articles are to be ground; then add 6 gallons of water at 144° of Fahrenheit, stir well together, let stand for 1 1/2 hour; draw off the liquor as much as possible. Repeat the same operation with 3 gallons for the 2d and 3d time ; mix these liquors, boil them ; clarify with the white of 1 or 2 eggs; cool as quick as possible to 50° of Fahrenheit (see No. 6); add ½ lb. of yeast, and fill up in casks when the fermentation is over.

291. Porter en Cercles.

11 pints of pale malt.

8 1/2 pints of yellow malt.

4 1/2 pints of brown malt.

Ground; macerate for 1 1/2 hour with 6 gallons of water at 144° of Fahrenheit (see No. 5); stir and mix it well; let it stand covered for 1 1/2 hour. Draw off the liquor as clear and as much as possible. Repeat a second or third time the same operation, only with 3 gallons each time. Mix these liquors; boil and clarify with the white of 1 or 2 eggs (see No. 6); add 3 ounces of hops and 1/2 drachm of salt; strain, and cool as quick as possible; add 1/2 pint of yeast at 50° of Fahrenheit; fill in cask, and let it ferment.

292. Punch, Imperial Raspberry Whiskey.

5 ounces of sweet almonds.

5 do. bitter do.

Infused in boiling water; then skin, and add 1 1/4 ounce of powdered cinnamon, ⅛ ounce of powdered cloves, and 5 ounces of plain syrup (see No. 7); rub them fine; boil in 2 gallons of water for 5 minutes; strain, add when cool 2 gallons of whiskey, and one gallon of raspberry syrup. (See No. 356.)

293. Punch, Kirschwasser. (Essence of.)

53 1/3 lbs. of white sugar.

3 1/3 gallons of water.

Boil to the crack (see Nos. 9 and 17); add 1 2/3 gallons of lemon juice; stir till getting clear, then put it id a clean tub, add when cold 5 gallons of kirschwasser. Filter. (See No. 3.)

294. Punch, d'Orsay.

24 lemons, the yellow rinds only.

24 oranges, do. do. do.

Cut; macerate for 24 hours with 4 gallons of fourth-proof brandy (see No. 5); then make a syrup of 12 lbs. of sugar boiled (see No. 7) with 6 gallons of water and the juice of 24 oranges and 12 lemons; skim and mix all together and filter. (See No. 3.)

295. Punch, Regent.

14 lemons, the rinds only.

14 oranges, do. do.

18 2/3 drachms of ground cinnamon.

⅔ do. do. cloves.

2 do. do. vanilla.

Cut; macerate for 24 hours with 2 gallons of pure Cognac, and 2 gallons of pure Jamaica rum (see No. 5). Strain, press, and add 12 lbs. of sugar, boiled with 6 gallons of water; skim, and add to the syrup 2 ounces of green tea; let it cool, and add the juice of 60 lemons and 14 oranges. Filter. (See No. 3.)

296. Punch, Roman.

The juice of 84 lemons must be beaten to a froth with 42 eggs; then add to it 1 1/2 gallon of boiling syrup, 1 1/2 gallon of Cognac, 1 1/2 gallon of Jamaica rum, 2 gallons of sherbet, maraschino (see No. 329), and 1 gallon of marasquino di Zara. (See No. 282.)

297. Punch, Rum.(Essence of.)

53 1/3 lbs. of sugar.

3 1/3 gallons of water.

Boiled to the crack (see Nos. 9 and 17); add 1 2⁄3 gallon of lemon juice (to the boiling sugar); stir till getting clear; then put in a clean tub, and when near cool add 5 gallons of good Jamaica rum. Filter. (See No. 3.)

298. Quatia.

1 lb. of quassia-root. 1 lb. of orange peel. Ground; macerate for 24 hours with 3 gallons of alcohol, 95 per cent., (see No. 5); strain, press; add 32 lbs. of sugar dissolved in 5 gallons of water. Filter. (See No. 3.)

299. Ratafia d'Abricots. (Ratafia of Apricots.)

8 1/2 lbs. of apricots, the juice of them; boil for 5 minutes in 20 lbs. of sugar, and 4 1⁄4 gallons of water; then add 4 gallons of alcohol, 95 per cent. Filter. (See No. 3.)

300. Ratafia d'Angelique. (Ratafia of Angelica.)

12 ounces of angelica-root, cut.

8 do. juniper berries, ground.

Macerate for 8 days with 4 gallons of alcohol, 95 per cent., and 20 lbs. of sugar dissolved in 4 3⁄4 gallons of water (see No. 5). Filter. (See No. 3.)

301. Ratafia d'Anis. (Ratafia of Anise-seed.)

6 3⁄4 ounces of green anise-seed.

13 1⁄2 do. star anise-seed.

Ground; macerate for 8 days in 4 gallons of alcohol, 95 per cent. (see No. 5); strain, press; add 20 lbs. of sugar dissolved in 4 3⁄4 gallons of water. Filter. (See No. 3.)

302. Ratafia de Cafe. (Ratafia of Coffee.)

10 lbs. of roasted Mocha coffee. Ground; macerate for 8 days in 4 gallons of alcohol, 95 per cent. (see No. 5); strain; add 20 lbs. of sugar dissolved in 4 3⁄4 gallons of water. Filter. (See No. 3.)

303. Ratafia de Cassis. (Ratafia of Black Currants.)

The juice of 12 lbs. of black currants, boiled for 5 minutes with 20 lbs. of sugar, and 4 1/2 gallons of water, then add 4 gallons of alcohol, 95 per cent. Filter. (See No. 3.)

304. Ratafia de Coings. (Ratafia of Quinces.)

49 quinces, grated.

Macerate for 8 days with 4 gallons of alcohol, 95 per cent. (see No. 5); press; add 20 lbs. of sugar dissolved in 4 3/4 gallons of water. Filter. (See No. 3.)

305. Ratafia de Fleurs d'Oranges. (Ratafia of Orange Flowers.)

4 1/2 lbs. of fresh orange flowers.

Macerate for 8 days with 4 gallons of alcohol, 95 per cent. (see No. 5); strain, press ; add ¾ of a gallon of double orange-flower water and 20 lbs. of sugar dissolved in 4 gallons of water. Filter. (See No. 3.)

306. Ratafia de Framboises. (Ratafia of Raspberries.)

12 lbs. of raspberries, the juice of them boiled for 5 minutes with 20 lbs. of sugar; dissolve in 4 1/2 gallons of water; strain, add 4 gallons of alcohol, 95 per cent. Filter. (See No. 3.)

307. Ratafia de Genievre. (Ratafia of Juniper.)

2 lbs. of juniper berries.

½ ounce of cinnamon.

1 do. coriander,

¼ do. mace.

Ground; macerate for 8 days with 4 gallons of alcohol, 95 per cent. (see No. 5); strain, add 20 lbs. of sugar dissolved in 4 3/4 gallons of water. Filter. (See No. 3.)

308. Ratafia de Grenades. (Ratafia of Pomegranates.)

105 pomegranates ripe, cut; macerate for 8 days in 4 gallons of alcohol, 95 per cent. (see No. 5); strain, press, add 20 lbs. of sugar dissolved in 4 ¾ gallons of water. Filter. (See No. 3.)

309. Ratafia de Grenoble.

½ ounce of Ceylon cinnamon.

1/4 do. cloves.

1/4 do. mace.

1 1/2 lb. of cherry-leaves.

8 lbs. of black cherries.

Ground; macerate for 8 days with 4 gallons of alcohol, 95 per cent. (see No. 5); add 20 lbs. of sugar dissolved in 5 gallons of black wild-cherry juice. Filter. (See No. 3.)

310. Ratafia de Groseilles. (Ratafia of Currants.)

12 lbs. of red currants, the juice of them boiled for 5 minutes with 20 lbs. of sugar, dissolved in 4 1/4 gallons of water; strain, add 4 gallons of alcohol, 95 per cent. Filter (See No. 3.)

311. Ratafia de Mares. (Ratafia of Blackberries.)

Boil the juice of 12 lbs. of blackberries for 5 minutes, with 20 lbs. of sugar dissolved in 4 1/2 gallons of water; strain, and add 4 gallons of alcohol, 95 per cent. Filter. (See No. 3.)

312. Ratafia de Neuilly.

25 lbs. of sour cherries (red with small stems).

10 lbs. of black cherries.

5 lbs. of red pinks.

Made to a pulp without breaking stones; macerate for 2 weeks with 4 1/4 gallons of alcohol, 95 per cent. (see No. 5); strain, press, and add one gallon of syrup and water up to 10 gallons.

313. Ratafia de Noix. (Ratafia of Walnuts.)

420 unripe walnuts (in month of August.)

4 1⁄3 drachms of cloves.

4 1⁄3 do. mace.

4 1/3 do. Ceylon cinnamon.

Ground and mashed; macerate for 2 weeks with 4 gallons of alcohol, 95 per cent., and 3 1⁄2 gallons of water (see No. 5); strain, press and add gallons of white plain syrup (see No. 7). Filter. (See No. 3.)

314. Ratafia de Noyaux. (Ratafia of Noyau.)

3 1⁄4 lbs. of apricot kernels ground; macerate for 2 weeks with 4 gallons of alcohol, 95 per cent. (see No. 5); strain, press, and then add 20 lbs. of sugar dissolved in 4 3⁄4 gallons of water. Filter. (See No. 3.)

315. Ratafia de Oillets. (Ratafia of Pinks)

16 lbs. of pinks, the flower-leaves only.

1 ounce of Ceylon cinnamon.

1 do. cloves.

Ground; macerate for 2 weeks with 4 gallons of alcohol, 95 per cent., and 3 1⁄2 gallons of water (see No. 5); strain, press, and add 2 1⁄2 gallons of white plain syrup. Filter.

316. Ratafia de Peaches. (Ratafia of Peaches.)

12 lbs. of peaches (the juice of them).

Let the liquid ferment for 8 days; break the stones, and add to it a syrup made of 20 lbs. of sugar boiled for 5 minutes with 4 1⁄4 gallons of water; then add 4 gallons of alcohol, 95 per cent. Filter.

317. Ratafia de Quatre Fruits. (Ratafia of Pour Pruits.)

1 gallon of black cherry juice.

1 do. red currant do.

1 do. black do. do.

1 do. raspberry do.

½ an ounce of ground cloves,

½ do. coriander-seed.

Macerate for 1 week with 4 gallons of alcohol, 95 per cent. (see No. 5); add 24 lbs. of sugar moistened and boiled with ½ a gallon of water; mix boiling hot. Filter.

318, Ratafia de Sept Graines. (Ratafia of Seven Seeds.)

8 ounces of dill-seed.

3 do. angelica-seed.

8 ounces of fennel-seed.

3 do. coriander-seed.

3 do. carrot-seed.

3 do. caraway-seed.

3 do. green anise-seed.

Ground; macerate for 8 days with 4 gallons of alcohol, 95 per cent,, and 3 1⁄2 gallons of water (see No. 5); add 2 1⁄2 gallons of white plain syrup. Filter. (See Nos. 3 and 7.)

319. Rosa Bianca. (White Rose.)

40 drops of oil of roses.

65 do. tincture of musk.

Dissolved in 3 gallons of alcohol, 95 per cent.; add 20 lbs. of sugar dissolved in 5 ¾ gallons of water. Filter.

320. Rose Rouge. (Red Rose.)

40 drops of oil of roses.

40 do. tincture of musk.

24 do. oil of orange.

Dissolved in 3 gallons of alcohol, 95 per cent., and add 20 lbs. of sugar dissolved in 5 3/4 gallons of water, and color rose. (See No. 93.) Filter. (See No. 3.)

321. Rosolio.

2 drachms of essence of vanilla.

13 drops of oil of roses.

57 do. essence of amber.

Dissolved in 3 gallons of alcohol, 95 per cent., and add 20 lbs. of sugar dissolved in 5 3/4 gallons of water; color rose. (See No. 93.) Filter.

322. Rosolio de Breslau.

2 drachms of essence of vanilla.

16 drops of oil of roses.

24 do. oil of neroly.

9 oranges, the juice of.

Add 4 lbs. of dried figs, cut; boil the orange juice and figs together for 5 minutes in a boiler containing 20 lbs. of sugar and 5 3/4 gallons of water; then press, strain, and add 3 gallons of alcohol, 95 per cent., having previously dissolved the essence and oils in it; color rose. (See No. 93.) Filter. (See No. 3.)

323. Ruga. (Rue.)

2 lbs. of ruga, or rue.

Macerate for 24 hours (see No. 5) with 3 gallons of alcohol, 95 per cent.; strain, press, and add 20 lbs. of sugar dissolved in 5 3/4 gallons of water. Filter. (See No. 3.)

324. Rum, Jamaica.

35 gallons of sugar scum, from refineries.

7 do. West India molasses.

Dissolved in 35 gallons of water hot enough to get the mixture at 80° (degrees) heat; add 1 gallon of good brewers' yeast. When fermentation is over distil and add 1/8 of a gallon of plain syrup (see No. 7); color with oak bark dark yellow.

325. Rum, Jamaica, Imitation.

7 lbs. of fragments of sugar canes.

Macerate (see No. 5) for 24 hours with 6 gallons of alcohol, 95 per cent., and 4 gallons of water; add 13 ounces of common salt; distil over 6 gallons of flavored spirit; add 3 3⁄4 gallons of water, ¼ of a gallon of white plain syrup (see No. 7); color dark yellow with oak bark.

326. Rum, St. Croix. (Santa Cruz Rum.)

62 lbs. of brown sugar dissolved in 40 gallons of boiling water; cool it down to 80° (degrees); add 1 gallon of brewers' yeast. When fermentation is over distil.

327. Sherbet, Currant.

2 1⁄2 gallons of currant juice.

2 do. fresh calves'-feet jelly.

2 do. currant wine.

2 do. currant ratafia.

24 lbs. of sugar dissolved in the juice. Filter warm. (See No. 3.)

328. Sherbet, Lemon.

2 1⁄2 gallons of lemon juice.

2 do. fresh calves'-feet jelly.

2 do. Madeira wine.

2 do. French brandy.

24 lbs. of sugar rubbed with the rinds of the lemons.
Filter warm. (See No. 3.)

329. Sherbet, Marasquino.

2 1⁄2 gallons of orange juice.

2 do. fresh calves'-feet jelly.

5 1⁄2 do. Marasquino di Zara. Filter warm. (See No. 3.)

330. Sherbet de Quatre Fruits. (Sherbet of Four Fruits.)

2 1⁄2 gallons of cherry juice.

2 do. fresh calves'-feet jelly.

5 do. ratafia de quatre fruits. Filter warm. (See No. 3).

331. Sherbet, Raspberry.

2 1/2 gallons of raspberry juice.
2 do. fresh calves'-feet jelly.
5 do. ratafia de framboises (raspberry).
Filter warm. (See No. 3.)

332. Sherbet, Rum.

2 1/2 gallons of lemon juice.
2 do. fresh calves'-feet jelly.
2 do. rum shrub.
2 do. Jamaica rum.
24 lbs. of sugar rubbed with the lemon rinds.
Filter warm. (See No. 3.)

333. Shrub, Currant.

5 5/8 gallons of red currant juice.
40 lbs. of sugar.
Boiled together for 8 or 10 minutes; let cool; add 1 1/2 gallons of good
French brandy. Filter. (See No. 3.)

334. Shrub, Lemon.

5 1/4 gallons of lemon cordial.
3 1/4 do. do. juice.
1 1/2 do. plain syrup (see No. 7).
Filter. (See No. 3.)

335. Shrub, Raspberry.

3 1/2 gallons of raspberry juice.
2 do. vinegar.
48 lbs. of sugar.

Boiled and skimmed for half an hour; when cold add 1 1/2 gallon of good French brandy. Filter. (See No. 3.)

336. Shrub, Rum.

4 gallons of proof Jamaica rum.

1 7/8 do. plain syrup (see No. 7).

3 3/4 do. lemon juice.

3/8 do. water.

Filter. (See No. 3.)

337. Soda Water.

10 gallons of water filled in a fountain receiver; add 8 1/3 ounces of crystallized citric acid; add 8 1/3 ounces of bicarbonate of soda in lumps or crystals; screw on the pipe quick; shake it to dissolve.

338. Spring Beer.

3 small bunches of sweet fern.

3 do. do. sarsaparilla.

3 do. do. winter green.

3 do. do. sassafras.

3 do. do. prince pine.

3 do. do. spice wood.

8 gallons of water boiled down to 6 gallons of decoction or extract; strain; 4 gallons of water boiled down to 3 gallons of decoction, with ½ a lb. of hops; strain; mix the two extracts or decoctions together; dissolve in them 1 gallon of molasses, and, when cooled to 80° (degrees) heat, 1 1/2 lb. of roasted bread soaked in fresh brewers' yeast; fill up a 10-gallon keg; when fermentation is over mix with it the white of one egg beaten to froth; bung it, and bottle when clear.

339. Spruce Beer.

9 1/2 gallons of water boiled; let it cool to 80° (degrees) heat, and then dissolve 9 lbs. of sugar in it, having previously mixed with it 1 ounce of essence of spruce; then add 1 pint of good brewers' yeast, and pour it in a

10-gallon keg till fermentation is over; then add a handful of brick powder
and the white of 2 eggs beaten to a froth; mix with the beer, and let it stand
till clear, then bottle.

340. Stomachic Beverage.

10 gallons of boiling water.

10 ounces of cream of tartar.

15 do. ground ginger.

10 lemons, cut in slices.

Macerate (see No. 5) together; let it stand till nearly cold; strain, press, and
dissolve in it 15 lbs. of sugar, previously rubbed together with ½ an ounce
of the oil of cloves and ½ an ounce of the oil of cinnamon; when nearly
lukewarm add 1 pint of yeast; let it stand for 14 hours; skim and filter;
bottle, and. be careful to bind the corks well.

341. Strong Sangaree.

¼ lb. of candied lemons.

1/4 do. do. oranges.

Cut very small; macerate them with 4 gallons of cherry brandy (see No. 5),
½ a gallon of lemon juice, and 1 gallon of Madeira wine for 8 days; strain
and press; then macerate in another demijohn, for the same length of time,
½ a lb. of grated nutmegs, a 1/2 lb. of powdered allspice, 2 ounces of
pounded bitter almonds, with 3 1/2 gallons of proof spirit; strain, press,
and mix the two extracts. Filter. (See No. 3.)

342. Syrup, Arrack Punch.

(For numerous other recipes for making syrups see Appendix)

53 1/3 lbs. of sugar.

3 1/3 gallons of water.

Boiled to the crack (see Nos. 9 and 17); add 1 2/3 gallons of lemon juice
(to the boiling sugar), and stir till the liquid is clear; pour it in a clean tub,
and, when nearly cool, add 5 gallons of Batavia arrack; then filter. (See
No. 421.)

343. Syrup, Blackberry.

80 lbs. of crushed sugar moistened and boiled for 2 minutes with 5 gallons of blackberry juice, skimmed and strained boiling hot. (See No. 421.)

344. Syrup of Coffee.

10 lbs. of fresh Java coffee, fresh roasted and ground.

6 gallons of boiling water.

Let it stand, well covered, till cool; strain and press; then dissolve in this infusion 80 lbs. of sugar; boil and skim for 2 minutes, and then strain. (See No. 421.)

345. Sirop de Cannelle. (Cinnamon Syrup.)

1 ounce of oil of Ceylon cinnamon.

Rubbed and dried up with carbonate of magnesia in a mortar, so as to make it a powder (see latter part of No. 3); put it in a filter bag, and pour 5 gallons of water on it; pour the water over and over till it runs clear; get in this way 5 gallons of clear high-flavored water; dissolve 80 lbs. of sugar in the flavored water, and boil for 2 minutes; then skim and strain. (See No. 421.)

346. Sirop Capillaire. (Maidenhair Syrup.)

1 lb. of maidenhair herb.

5 1/2 gallons of boiling water.

Macerate till cold (see No. 5); strain without pressing, so as to get 5 gallons; take the whites of 3 eggs beaten to froth, and mix them with the infusion; keep back a quart of the liquid; then dissolve and boil in the above 80 lbs. of sugar by a good heat; when the scum rises, put in a little from the quart of cold liquid, and this will make the scum settle; let it raise and settle 3 times; then skim, and when perfectly clear add ½ a pint of orange-flower water; then boil once up again and strain. (See No. 7.)

347. Sirop de Cerises. (Cherry Syrup.)

5 gallons of cherry juice.

Let it ferment a few days; dissolve and boil 80 lbs. of sugar; when clear, skim and strain. (See No. 7.)

348. Sirop de Groseilles. (Red Currant Syrup.)

5 gallons of currant juice, pressed after having fermented with the fruit for 2 days; dissolve and boil with 80 lbs. of sugar; skim till clear; then strain. (See Nos. 7 and 421.)

349. Sirop de Fleurs d'Oranges. (Syrup of Orange Flowers.)

5 gallons of orange-flower water boiled up for 2 minutes with 80 lbs. of sugar; skim and strain. (See Nos. 7 and 421.)

350. Sirop de Gomme. (Gum Syrup.)

20 lbs. of best clear white gum arabic dissolved in 4 gallons of water, nearly boiling hot; take 60 lbs. of sugar, melt and clarify it with 1 gallon of water (see Nos. 6 and 7); add the gum solution, and boil for 2 minutes. (See No. 421.)

351. Sirop de Limons. (Lemon Syrup.)

5 gallons of lemon juice.

1 ounce of best oil of lemons.

Dissolved in ½ a pint of alcohol, or the rinds of 16 lemons rubbed with sugar to extract the essential oil; dissolve 80 lbs. of sugar in the juice, and boil for 2 minutes; skim, then strain. (See Nos. 2 and 421.)

352. Sirop d'Oranges. (Orange Syrup.)

5 gallons of orange juice.

Take the rinds of 16 oranges, and rub them with loaf sugar to extract the essential oil; then take 80 lbs. of sugar and dissolve it in the juice; boil 2 minutes, skim, and strain. (See Nos. 7 and 421.)

353. Sirop d'Orgeat. (Orgeat Syrup.)

10 lbs. of sweet almonds.

4 lbs. of bitter almonds.

Cover them with boiling-hot water; let them stand till near cold, and peel them by pressing through your fingers; beat them in a stone or brass mortar to a very fine paste with some sugar, adding water slowly; press through a linen cloth, so as so get 5 gallons of liquid resembling rich milk; dissolve in this liquid 80 lbs. of sugar; boil up once, and add 1 pint of orange-flower water; then strain. (See Nos. 7 and 421.)

354. Sirop d'Ananas. (Pineapple)

5 gallons of pineapple juice, after fermenting 2 days with the fruit; dissolve in the juice 80 lbs of sugar, and boil for 2 minutes; skim and strain. (See Nos. 7 and 421.)

355. Syrup, Plain.

For a description how to make this syrup, see No. 7.

356. Syrup, Raspberry,

5 gallons of raspberry juice, after having fermented for 2 days; dissolve in it and boil for 2 minutes 80 lbs. of sugar; skim and strain; then filter. (See No. 7.)

357. Syrup, Raspberry Vinegar.

5 gallons of raspberry vinegar. (See No. 363.)

Dissolve in it 80 lbs. of sugar; boil for 2 minutes; skim and strain. (See Nos. 7 and 421.)

358. Syrup, Strawberry.

5 gallons of strawberry juice, after having fermented the fruit for 2 days; dissolve in it and boil for 2 minutes 80 lbs. of sugar; skim, and then strain. (See No. 7.)

359. Tickle my Fancy.

¼ gallon of lemon juice,

2 gallons of calves'-feet jelly.

8 lbs. of stoned raisins.

4 do. sugar.

Boiled together, with the addition of a little water, so as to get 2 1/2 gallons of liquid; press, strain, and add 4 gallons of good cider; also macerate for 24 hours (see No. 5) 8 ounces of ground cloves, 8 ounces of ground cinnamon, 1 lb. of ground ginger, ¼ of a pound of lemon peel cut, ¼ of a lb. of isinglass dissolved in a ¼ leak of a gallon of white wine, and 4 gallons of French brandy, 4th proof; strain, press; filter.

360. Usquebaugh.

1 1/4 lb. of cinnamon.

10 ounces of cloves.

10 do. nutmeg.

10 do. ginger.

10 do. allspice.

All ground and macerated for 8 days (see No. 5) with 10 gallons of old Irish whiskey; then make another tincture consisting of 2 1/2 ounces of Spanish saffron, 10 ounces of isinglass dissolved in 1 quart of white wine in another vessel; macerate both for the same length of time, say 8 days; then strain both tinctures; then dissolve 8 lbs. of sugar candy in ½ a gallon of water ; strain, and mix all these three strained liquids together, and add 5 ounces of tincture of rhubarb. Filter. (See No. 3.)

361. Verdulino de Turino.

1 ounce of myrrh.

4 ounces of Ceylon cinnamon.

4 ounces of cardamom.

Macerate for 24 hours (see No. 5) with 3 1/2 gallons of alcohol, 95 per cent., and 4 gallons of water; distil from off the water 3 1/2 gallons of flavored spirit, and add 24 lbs. of sugar dissolved in 5 gallons of water; color green. (See No. 90.) Filter.

362. Vespetro.

8 ounces of angelica-seed.

4 do. Ceylon cinnamon.

1 do. mace.

40 lemons, the yellow rinds only.

Macerate for 24 hours (see No. 5) with 3 1/2 gallons of alcohol, 95 per cent., and 4 gallons of water; distil from off the water 3 1/2 gallons of flavored spirit, and add 24 lbs. of sugar dissolved in 5 gallons of water. Filter. (See No. 3.)

363. Vinegar, Raspberry.

30 lbs. of raspberries made to a pulp.

7 1/2 gallons of wine or cider vinegar.

Macerate for 8 days (see No. 5); press and strain.

364. Whiskey, Irish.*

3 gallons of genuine Irish whiskey.

7 do. best pure spirit, mixed.

* Without large distilleries these whiskers —Irish and Scotch (see Scotch, Nos. 364-366)—cannot be manufactured with profit. It is a humbug to make them with essences, and a nuisance as regards health. The best imitation is mixing in proportion to the price.

365. Whiskey, Monongahela.

3 gallons of Monongahela whiskey.

7 do. pure spirit.

Color yellow. (See No. 91.)

366. Whiskey, Scotch.

3 gallons of best genuine Scotch whiskey.

7 do. best pure spirit. Mix.

367. Wine, Blackberry.

½ ounce of ground cinnamon.

¼ do. do. cloves.

½ drachm of cardamom.

1 do. nutmug.

5 gallons of blackberries, made to a pulp. Mix with 5 gallons of water heated at 100° Fahrenheit, in which 10 lbs. of sugar have been previously dissolved; fill up a 10-gallon keg, but keep back ½ a gallon, and place it in a warm atmosphere; keep the keg constantly full from this ½ gallon, and after fermentation has ended strain and press; then add 1 gallon of alcohol, 95 per cent., and filter or fine. (See Findings, Nos. 202, 203, 204, and 205.)

368. Wine, Black Currant.

5 gallons of black currants, made to a pulp; mix with 5 gallons of water heated to 100° Fahrenheit, in which 10 lbs. of sugar have been previously dissolved; fill up a 10-gallon keg, but keep back ½ a gallon; put the keg in a warm place; keep it constantly full from the ½ gallon; strain, press, and then add 1 gallon of good alcohol, 95 per cent. Filter or fine. (See Findings, Nos. 202, 203, 204, and 205.)

369. Wine, Bordeaux, Red.

4 gallons of high-flavored red Bordeaux wine.

6 do. plain wine. Colored to the same shade with tincture of alderberries.

370. Wine, Bordeaux, White.

4 gallons of high-flavored white wine.

6 do. plain wine.

Color to the shade with coloring or tincture of saffron. (See Nos. 88 and 91.)

371. Wine, Birch.

9 gallons of birch juice, drawn in the month of February or March from the birch tree by boring holes in it; boil and skim, and cool it down to 100° Fahrenheit; then dissolve in it 9 lbs. of sugar, and add 2 ounces of lemon peels, finely cut; produce fermentation with 1 pint of gluten; put the ingredients in a keg, and keep it constantly full till fermentation is over; filter or fine it (see from Nos. 202 to 205), and put in another keg, in which you have previously burnt a strip of brimstone paper. (See No. 418.)

372. Wine, Champagne.

10 gallons of light white wine, such as Sauterne or Rhine wine, well clarified; add 3 lbs. of the whitest rock candy, dissolved in 1 1/2 pint of water; to this syrup add ½ a gallon of wine alcohol (bonjoût) or any other perfectly free of flavor; when all this is perfectly clear, fill it in a soda-water apparatus, and impregnate it with carbonic acid (for family use 1 1/2 drachm of citric acid, and 1 1/2 of bicarbonate of soda); bottle, cork, wire, cap and label.

373. Wine, Champagne, English.

5 gallons of currant juice.

5 do. water, in which 15 lbs. of sugar have been dissolved; let the liquid settle for 3 days, decant, and then add 1 1/4 gallon of pure spirit, free of flavor; put it in a keg, and let it stand unbunged for 6 weeks; bung up tight, let it stand for a year, and then bottle.

374. Wine, Cherry.

Take 10 gallons of fresh-pressed cherry juice, and dissolve it in 5 lbs. of sugar; put this juice in a keg, and keep it constantly full of the liquid during the process of fermentation; then filter or fine it (see from Nos. 202 to 205), and fill in a pitched keg or bottle.

375. "Wine, Currant, Red.

8 lbs. of honey.

10 do. sugar.

7 1/3 gallons of water boiled; clarified with the white of 1 egg; skim and strain; then add 1 3/8 gallon of red currant juice, and 1 pint of yeast; put in a keg, and keep it full of the liquid during fermentation; filter or fine (see from Nos. 202 to 205); put in a clean pitched keg, and bung tight or bottle.

376. Wine, Cyprus, Imitation of.

8 ⅔ gallons of water.

8 2/3 pints of alderberries.

7 3/8 lbs. of sugar.

7 drachms of ground ginger.

3 1/2 do. cloves.

Boil together for 1 hour; skim; strain when cooled to 100° Fahrenheit, and put in a 10-gallon keg which contains 10 1/2 ounces of mashed raisins; fill up the keg, and add 1 pint of yeast, and during fermentation be careful and keep the keg full with the balance of the liquid; filter or fine it. (See Nos. 202, 203, 204, and 205.)

377. Wine, Damson.

80 lbs. of damsons.

Macerate for 2 days (see No. 5) with 10 gallons of boiling water; strain, press, and dissolve 25 lbs. of sugar in the liquid; then add 2 1/2 pints of French brandy, and let it stand a few days; filter, bottle, and be careful and add ½ an ounce of ground sugar to each bottle; cork and string it.

378. Wine, Frontignan of.

4 1/2 gallons of red wine.

4 1/2 do. white wine.

1 do. 4th-proof spirit. Mix.

379. Wine, Ginger.

12 gallons of water and 19 lbs. of sugar dissolved and boiled to syrup (see No. 7), 9 ounces of washed and cut ginger, ½ a gallon of boiling water; macerate till cold (see No. 5); strain, press, and mix with the syrup; then

add 6 lbs. of Malaga raisins, 3 lbs. of Muscat raisins mashed to a pulp, 1 ounce of isinglass soaked in a pint of water, 4 lemons cut in slices, and 1 pint of good brewers' yeast; put all in a keg, and keep it full with the liquid during the process of fermentation for 3 weeks; at the end of which time bottle or fill a keg in which has been burned some brimstone; bang tight.

(See No. 418.)

380. Wine Grapes.

11 gallons of lightly-pressed juice of sweet grapes; fill a 10-gallon keg to the bung; let it stand in a warm place, and keep it full during fermentation; after it has settled draw it off in a clean keg; filter the dregs of the first, and add the clear to the liquid that has been drawn off. In the month of March the second fermentation begins, then lift the bung; when the second fermentation is over, if the wine is red, fine with the white of 1 egg beaten to a froth, but when white, with a mixture composed of 1 ounce of isinglass steeped in a pint of the wine, and beaten and mixed as with the egg; put the red wine in a pitched keg, the white in a brimstone keg, and bung tight.

381. Wine, Greek.

Take a sufficient quantity of perfectly ripe grapes to make 10 gallons of juice, and expose them to the sun for ten days; press out the juice in a boiler, and keep it over a fire until it attains the boiling point; then add 5 ozs. of sea-salt; take it from the fire, and let it stand for 8 days, then bottle.

382. Wine, Juniper.

12 1/2 gallons of hot water.

½ ounce of ground coriander-seed.

55 lbs. of ground juniper berries and

5 lbs. of brown sugar.

When the liquid is cooled to 100° Fahrenheit, add 1 pint of good brewers' yeast, and put all in a keg with the top out; fix the top again as tight as possible, and when fermentation is over, and the wine clear, draw off; press and filter the balance, and put it in a new, clean pitched keg.

383. Wine, Lemon.

Take 11 gallons of water and 15 lbs. of sugar, and boil them together until the sugar is perfectly dissolved; then skim and strain the liquid, and when it has cooled to 100° Fahrenheit, add 50 lemons, cut in very thin slices, and 1 quart of fresh brewers' yeast; put a 10-gallon keg in a warm place, and fill it full to the bung, and keep it full with the liquid during the fermentation; strain, press, and filter; then add ½ a gallon of good sherry, or Madeira wine.

384. Wine, Liqueur. (Cordial.)

Take a sufficient quantity of sweet grapes to make 2 gallons of juice, and expose them to the sun for 10 days before pressing them; as soon as they are pressed put the juice in a 10-gallon keg, and fill it up with 3 gallons of alcohol, 95 per cent., and 1 ounce of ground cinnamon; mix well, bung it, and after settling (say 1 month) bottle it.

385. Wine, Madeira.

4 gallons of good Madeira, high flavored.
6 do. plain wine.
Color to same shade with coloring or tincture of saffron (See Nos. 88 and 91.)

386. Wine, Malaga.

4 gallons of Malaga wine, best quality.
6 do. plain wine; and for sweetening add
2 1⁄2pints of plain syrup. (See No. 7.)
Color with elderberry tincture and coloring. (See 88.)

387. Wine, Mixed,

1 3⁄4 gallon of fresh-pressed currant juice.
1 3⁄4 do. do. do. grape do.
1 3⁄4 do. do. do. raspberry do.
1 3⁄4 do. do. do. Eng. cherry do.

24 lbs. of sugar dissolved in the mixed juices; add 1 quart of good brewers' yeast, and fill up a keg holding 8 gallons; keep the cask full with the remaining juice during fermentation; when this is over add 1 1/2 gallon of good French brandy; let it stand together for a few days - longer; then filter and bottle.

388. "Wine, Muscat. 10 gallons of plain wine. 20 lbs. of Muscat raisins, bruised. ¾ lb. alder-flowers, hanging in a bag. Macerate for 2 or 3 months (see No. 5); press, and filter or fine. (See Nos. 202, 203, 204, and 205.)

389. Wine, Orange.

11 gallons of water and 15 lbs. of sugar; boil, skim, and strain, and, when cooled to 100° Fahrenheit, add 50 oranges cut in thin slices, and 1 quart of fresh brewers' yeast; fill a keg to the bung, and keep it full with the liquid during fermentation, and let it stand in a warm place; when fermentation is over, strain, press, and add ½ a gallon of brandy. Filter. (See No. 3.)

390. Wine, Parsnip.

Boil 40 lbs. of parsnips and 11 gallons of water down to, 9 gallons; press out the liquid, beat 3 eggs to froth, and mix with the decoction; when it is cool take out ½ a gallon, and add 1 ounce of bruised bitter almonds, and dissolve in the decoction 25 lbs. of sugar; boil, and let the scum rise 3 times; then stop the raising by adding from the ½ gallon of cool liquid (see No. ;skim, strain, and cool down to 100° Fahrenheit; then add 1 quart of yeast, and, after fermentation is over, add quart 4th-proof Cognac. Filter. (See No. 3.)

391. Wine, Peach.

To 10 gallons of peach juice, pressed from the ripest fruits, add the stones, but without breaking them; dissolve 5 lbs. of sugar in the juice, and put it in a keg, which must be kept constantly full with the liquid till fermentation ends; then add 1 ounce of ground cloves, strain, and mix to it ½ a gallon of good pure alcohol, 95 per cent. Filter. (See No. 3.)

392. Wine, Plain.

9 1/2 gallons of water, at 86° Fahrenheit.

10 lbs. of sugar.

4 do. raisins, mashed.

3 ounces of tartaric acid.

1 pint of strong vinegar.

1 quart of brewers' yeast.

Mixed and dissolved together; fill up a keg, put it in a warm place, and keep it constantly full with the liquid until fermentation is over; then add 1 gallon of alcohol, 95 per cent.; strain, press, and filter. (See No. 3.)

393. Wine, Port.

4 gallons of high-flavored port wine.

5 5/8 gallons of plain wine.

⅜ do. plain syrup. (See No. 7.)

Colored with tincture of alderberries.

394. Wine, Quince.

8 gallons of quince juice, made as follows:

After wiping off the quinces cut them in slices and make a pulp; press out the juice; heat it near boiling; dissolve 10 lbs. of sugar in it; then skim, strain, and let it cool to 86° Fahrenheit; fill a keg, and put it in a warm place; add 1 quart of brewers' yeast; mix well; fill up the keg with the liquid during fermentation, and when over add 2 1/2 gallons of good sherry or Madeira wine. (See No. 3.)

395. Wine, Raisin.

Take 80 lbs. of Malaga raisins, and macerate with 10 gallons of boiling-water until cool (see No. 5); then rub them between the hands so as not to hurt the stones; pass the pulp through a sieve; press slowly, so as to get 11 gallons of the liquid with the water used to wash out the pulp; then dissolve in it 6 ounces of powdered rock candy, and add the rinds of 4 oranges, 2 lemons, and 1 ounce of bruised bitter almonds, with 1 quart of brewers' yeast; fill a 10-gallon keg, and keep it full with the liquid during fermentation; then strain, press, and add 1 quart of the best French brandy.

396. Wine, Raspberry.

Take 10 gallons of fresh raspberry juice, and add 7 1/2 lbs. of sugar, boiled and clarified with the white of 2 eggs; skim, strain, and when nearly cool add 1 pint of good brewers' yeast; fill a 10-gallon keg, and hang in it a little bag with 1 ounce of ground mace; fill up with the juice until fermentation is over, and add 1¼ gallon of good port wine. Filter. (See No. 3.)

397. Wine, Rose.

10 gallons of water.

30 lbs. of sugar.

1 1/4 gallon of red rose leaves.

Boil for 2 minutes; when lukewarm fill up a keg; put it in a warm place; add 1 pint of yeast; fill up constantly with the liquid till fermentation ceases; dissolve ½ drachm of otto of roses in 2 ounces of alcohol, 95 per cent., and mix it with the above wine; strain; color rose with the tincture of cochineal. Filter. (See Nos. 3 and 93.)

398. Wine, St. George.

5 gallons of dark red claret.

5 do. piquepouil.

Mix; add 1 gill of spirit of raspberries, 1 gill of spirit of lemonbalm, and 1 gill of spirit of orris-root.

399. Wine, Sherry.

4 gallons of high-flavored sherry wine.

6 do. plain wine.

Colored with coloring. (See No. 88.)

400. Wine, Tokay.

4 gallons of tokay, best quality.

6 do. plain wine.

Sugar and color to suit the taste.

APPENDIX.

CONTAINING DIFFERENT ARTICLES USUALLY KEPT FOE
USE IN LIQUOR STORES.

401. Bottle-wax, Black.

1 lb. of rosin, white and transparent; melt it in a tin dish over a slow fire; add about 1/2 an ounce of boiled linseed oil (varnish), so as when a drop is taken out on a cold stone it loses its brittleness; then add 1 ounce of lamp-black, stirred in until all lumps are dissolved.

402. Bottle-wax, Green.

1 lb. of rosin, white and transparent; melt it in a tin dish over a slow fire; add about 1/2 an ounce of boiled linseed oil (varnish), so as when a drop is taken out on a cold stone it loses its brittle quality; then mix in 4 ounces of chrome green, stirred until the lumps are dissolved.

403. Bottle-wax, Yellow.

1 lb. of rosin, white and transparent; melt it in a tin dish over a slow fire; add about 1/2 an ounce of boiled linseed oil or varnish, so as when a drop is taken out on a cold stone it loses its brittle character; then mix in 4 ounces of chrome yellow, finely powdered; stir until all lumps are dissolved.

404, Bottle-wax, Red,

1 lb. of rosin, white and transparent; melt it in a tin dish over a slow fire; add about ½ an ounce of boiled linseed oil or varnish, so as when a drop is taken out on a cold stone it loses its brittleness; then mix in 1 ounce of cinnabar or vermilion, mixed with 3 ounces of prepared chalk; stir until all lumps are dissolved.

405. Bottle-wax, White.

1 lb. of rosin, white and transparent; melt it in a tin dish over a slow fire; add about ½ an ounce of boiled linseed oil or varnish, so as when a drop is taken out on a cold stone it loses its brittleness; then mix in 4 ounces of zinc white; stir until all lumps are dissolved.

406. Brandy Apricots.

Take some nice apricots before becoming perfectly ripe, rub them slightly with a linen cloth, and prick them with a pin to the stone in different places ; then lay them in very cold water, and at the same time take equal parts of water and plain syrup, so as to cover the apricots ; boil the syrup in a copper boiler, and when boiling throw all the apricots at once in the syrup, and keep them down with the skimmer; when they begin to get soft under pressure of the finger, take them gently out, lay them in a sieve to drip off the syrup ; then arrange the fruit in an earthen dish, clarify the syrup with the white of an egg (see No. 7), boil it to its regular thickness, and throw it boiling hot on the apricots so as to cover them; let them stand for 24 hours, then take them out of the syrup, and put them in glass jars, without squeezing them. The balance of syrup is clarified again, and mixed with 3 parts white 4th-proof brandy; fill up the jars with syrup, and cork and seal them.

407. Brandy, Angelica.

Take thick, fresh angelica stems ; cut and free the stems of the leaves; wipe them clean with a linen cloth; make pieces of 1 to 1 1/2 inches in length, and put them in fresh water to be washed ; then put them in boiling water; boil up for several times; let the fire go out; cover the boiler; macerate for 1 hour; take them out with the skimmer, and put them in cold water; take them out again; press them gently between the linen cloth, so as to get all the water out; then boil them thoroughly in plain syrup, and lay them on a sieve to drip off the syrup for 24 hours; then again boil the syrup to its former thickness, clarify it, and mix it with 2 parts white 4th-proof brandy; fill up the jars, and cork and seal them.

408. Brandy Cedrats.

Take cedrats with very thick rinds; cut off, with a very sharp knife, the outside part of them, without touching the white; keep the rinds for the use of cordials, &c.; split the white rind in 4 parts, without touching the fruit; take the rinds off; put them for a little while in alum water (this is done to retain the natural color of the fruit); then boil in plain syrup by a slow fire, and when soft enough take them out with a skimmer; put them in an earthen dish; cover them with fresh clarified syrup; after 24 hours take them out of the dish, and put them in jars; mix 2 parts of white 4th-proof brandy (macerated before with some rinds); add 1 part of the syrup; fill up the jars, cork and seal.

409. Brandy Cherries.

6 lbs. of red sour cherries with short stems; take off the last; cover them with 1 gallon of 4th-proof white brandy; macerate them for 2 weeks (see No. 5); decant the liquor; then add 4 lbs. of sugar, moistened and boiled with 1 pint of water; skim; this done, make a tincture of 1 drachm of ground cloves, 4 drachms of ground coriander, 4 drachms of star anise, 2 drachms of ground cinnamon, and 36 grains of mace, with 1 quart of 4th-proof white brandy mixed with the above; filter; cover the cherries in the jars; cork and seal.

410. Brandy Grapes.

Take some Muscat grapes; pick out the soundest and largest fruit; wash and put them in cold water; prick them 2 or 3 times with a pin, and place them in a sieve to drip off the water; wipe dry with a linen the jars.

411. Brandy Melons.

Get some musk or other melons; cut them in slices; take the rind and the inside parts off; put them in water containing a little lemon juice, and boil them up for 2 or 3 times; take them off the fire; let them stand covered for 1 hour; then pour them in other cold water containing lemon juice, and let them cool; empty them on a sieve to drip off the water; then boil them gently in plain syrup (see No. 7); when soft take them off with the skimmer, and place them in an earthen dish; cover them with the fresh boiling clarified syrup, after 24 hours' standing; then drip off the syrup and arrange them in jars; clarify the syrup again; when necessary, mix with it 4th-proof white brandy, of 2 parts of its own volume; fill the jars up to cover the melons; cork and seal.

412. Brandy Mirabelles. (Plums.)

Get 6 lbs. of mirabelles ; rub them off with a linen cloth; prick them on the place of the stem, and opposite; cover them with 1 gallon of 4th-proof white brandy; macerate them for 2 weeks (see No. 7); decant the liquor; then add 4 lbs. of sugar moistened and boiled with 1 pint of water, and skim; this done, make a tincture of 1 drachm of ground cloves, 4 drachms of ground coriander-seed, 4 drachms of ground star anise-seed, 2 drachms of ground cinnamon, and 36 grains of ground mace, with 1 quart of 4th-proof white brandy, mixed with the above; filter; cover the mirabelles in jars, and cork and seal them.

413. Brandy Oranges.

Get, if possible, Havana oranges; cut off the yellow skin, and put it aside; peel off the white, and throw it away; prick the fruit with a pin, and then lay them in cold water; pour them at once in boiling water; boil up twice (about 1 minute); take off the fire; let them stand covered for 1 hour; put them in coldcloth, and arrange them in jars; cover them with the juice of the smaller fruit, mixed with 2 parts of white 4th-proof brandy, sweetened with plain syrup to taste, and filter; cork and seal water again, and after the water is dripped off, place them in a jar; then boil plain syrup and cover the oranges, and let them stand for 24 hours; drip off the syrup, and boil it to its regular consistence; repeat it twice more; after the third repetition drip off the syrup; clarify it with the white of eggs (see No. 7); mix it with 2 parts white 4th-proof brandy; filter, and cover the oranges with it in jars; cork and seal.

414. Brandy Peaches.

Take some nice peaches a little before being perfectly ripe; rub them off slightly with a linen cloth; prick them with a pin to the stones in different places, and put them in cold water; at the same time take equal parts of water and plain syrup (see No. 7) in quantity sufficient to cover the peaches in a copper boiler; when the syrup boils throw in the peaches; keep them down with the skimmer, until soft; take them out, lay them on a sieve to drip off the syrup; next clarify the syrup with the white of eggs; boil it to the proper thickness, and then arrange the peaches in an earthen dish, and throw it boiling hot over them, so as to cover them; Jet them stand for 24 hours; fill them in jars, without squeezing; then again clarify the balance of the syrup, and mix it with 3 parts of 4th-proof white brandy; fill up the jars; cork and seal them.

415. Brandy Pears.

Take small, highly-perfumed pears, skin them, taking care not to damage the stems; cut off the ends of the stems and lay the fruit in iron-free alum water (by this means you retain the natural color of the fruit); let them remain in for an hour; take them out, and put them in boiling water; as soon as they get soft take them out, and lay them in cold water which contains the juice of a few lemons; when the water becomes warm it must be changed with cold; when perfectly cold arrange them in jars, without breaking the stems; take, in the beginning of the operation, 1 part of boiling hot syrup, and throw it over the skins; let it cool; then add 2 parts of 4th-proof white brandy; mix it with the syrup; filter, and fill the jars up; cork and seal.

416. Brandy Prunes, or Plums,

Are made precisely the same way as the peach.

417. Brandy Quinces.

Rub the quinces with a linen cloth, and take off the skin very delicately, and lay them in cold water; cut them in 4 parts; take out the hearts; then lay them in iron-free alum water for a few minutes (by this means you retain the natural color of the fruit), and throw them in boiling syrup until they begin to get soft; take them out with the skimmer; arrange them in an earthen dish; clarify the syrup ; throw it boiling hot on the fruit to cover; after 24 hours' standing drip off the syrup; clarify it, and add 2 parts of 4th-proof white brandy, in which were macerated the skins of the fruit; filter, and fill up the jars previously arranged with the quinces; cork and seal.

418. Brimstone Paper, for smoking Kegs, to prevent "Wine getting sour.

1 lb. of brimstone melted in an iron pan.

40 to 50 strong paper strips, of an inch in breadth and 9 inches long, are drawn through the melted brimstone and laid aside; when all done, repeat it a second and third time to get the thickness of good-sized pasteboard; some take ground coriander-seed, anise-seed, and fennel-seed, equal parts mixed together, which they strew, after the last dipping, on the brimstone paper strips while hot; they are packed in bundles of a of a lb., with strings on both ends, and brought into market. Use.—Take for a 60-gallon cask 1 strip; light it with a match; bring it to the bunghole; put the bung loosely in; let it burn as long as it can; let the cask stand untouched for 1 hour; then take it out, and put in the white wine; red wine would lose its color.

419. Mustard, French,

1½ lb. of ground black mustard-seed.

1 1/2 do. do. yellow do. do.

3 quarts of good strong boiling hot cider vinegar.

Mixed thoroughly together; macerate 12 hours; add ounce of ground allspice, ½ an ounce of ground ginger, 3 ounces of sea-salt, 1 1/2 ounce of ground cinnamon, ½ an ounce of ground cloves; mix it well with the above; add as much more vinegar as to get the required consistency.

420. Wax Putty, for Leaky Casks, Bungs, Corks, &c. 2 lbs. of spirits of turpentine. 4 do. tallow. 8 do. yellow wax. 12 do. solid turpentine. The wax and solid turpentine are melted together on a slow fire; then add the

tallow; when melted take it far off from the fire; then stir in the spirit of turpentine, and let it cool.

421. General Directions for Syrups.

The best syrups can only be made with the finest qualities of sugar. Syrup is the juice of fruit, flowers, vegetables, or whatever you desire to preserve, mixed with liquid sugar. In boiling to the degrees, it is from the "small thread" (see No. 10) to the "large pearl" (see No. 13) that syrup is produced. The essences or virtues of most fruits, &c., suitable for syrup-making may be extracted by simple infusion. The sugar should be dissolved in this decoction or infusion, and both placed in a glass or earthenware vessel; close this vessel down, and place it in a pan on the fire surrounded with water. In some cases the syrup should not be bottled till quite cold. When ready, cork it securely, and stand it in a cool dry place.

Care should be taken to boil the syrup to the precise point. If not sufficiently boiled, after a time it is apt to become mouldy; and if boiled too much, it will grain a little, and thus become candied. Saucepans made of tin, or tinned on the inside, should not be used when making syrups from red fruits, as these act on the tin, and turn the color to a dead blue.

(See Nos. 6 and 7.)

422. Raspberry Syrup.

2 pints of filtered raspberry juice.

4¼ lbs. of sugar.

Select the fruit, either white or red. Having picked them over, mash them in a pan, which put in a warm place until fermentation has commenced. Let it stand for about three days. All mucilaginous fruits require this, or else they would jelly when bottled. Now filter the juice through a close flannel bag, or blotting-paper, and add sugar in the proportion mentioned above ; this had better be powdered. Place the syrup on the fire, and as it heats skim it carefully, but don't let it boil; or you may mix in a glass vessel or earthenware jar, and place in a pan of water on the fire. This is a very clean way, and prevents the sides crusting and burning. When dissolved to the "little pearl" (see No. 12) take it off; strain through a cloth; bottle when cold; cover with tissue-paper dipped in brandy, and tie down with a bladder.

423. Currant Syrup.
2 pints of currant juice.
4¼ lbs. of sugar.

Take as many currants (which can be mixed, white and red) as you think sufficient (about 6 lbs.), and pick them over. Now mash and ferment, as in the instructions for making raspberry syrup (see No. 422). This done, add some raspberries, and flavor as you please. Some mix a pound of raspberries and a pound of cherries (properly stoned before mashing); then mix, mash, and ferment all together. The quantity of raspberries to be introduced, however, is entirely a matter of taste. Whilst the syrup is fermenting, it is a good plan to cover the pan with a coarse cloth, or any thing that will admit the air (which is essential to fermentation), but keep out the dust.

424. Orgeat (or Almond) Syrup.

2 lbs. of sweet almonds.
3 1/2 ounces of bitter almonds.
3 pints of fresh water.
6 or 6 1/2 lbs. of sugar.

Take your almonds (sweet and bitter) and drop them into boiling water. This blanches them, and they are easily skinned. Having peeled them, drop them into cold water, in which wash them; when ready put them into a clean mortar (one of marble is better than bronze), and mash them; next, squeeze in the juice of two lemons, or add a little acid, and, as you pound the almonds, pour part of a pint of clean water into the mortar; mash thoroughly, until the mixture looks like thick milk, and no pieces of almonds are left; then add another pint of the spring water. Now squeeze the white mash through a hair-cloth, or other good strainer: a common plan is to have a large strainer held by two persons; as they twist the milk may be caught in a clean basin; whatever of the almonds is left in the cloth put it back into the mortar, and mash it over again, adding a little of the spring water; then strain it, and mix with the former almond milk; this done mix it with your sugar (about 6 lbs.) which must first, however, be clarified and boiled to a "crack" (see No. 17); whilst adding the almond milk let the pan of hot sugar be off the fire; when mixed give another boil up; then remove the pan from the fire, and stir the syrup until cold ;* pour in a small portion of the tincture of orange flowers, or the least drop of the essence of neroly, and pass the mixture again through a cloth; give the bottles an occasional shake for a few days afterward; it will keep the syrup from parting.

* This is done to keep it from separating and splitting up after being bottled.

425. Morello Cherry Syrup.

2 lbs. of Morello cherries.

4 lbs. of sugar.

See that the cherries are ripe, and, having stoned them, mash them in a colander or sieve, pressing out the juice into a pan or basin; let the juice stand for a day or two, then strain through a flannel bag until very clear; boil your clarified sugar to a " crack" (see No. 17), and pour the juice in, in the proportion of one pint of juice to 2 lbs. of sugar; stir it well on the fire with a skimmer, and give it one or two boils; if any scum rises take it off; let it thoroughly cool; then bottle off, or put them in deep jars, and tie down with bladders.

426. Mulberry Syrup.

2 pints of mulberry juice.

2 3/4 lbs. of sugar.

Mulberries do not require so much sugar as raspberries (see No. 422). Mash the mulberries, and proceed as with cherry syrup (see No. 425). See that the mulberries are uniformly ripe.

427. Strawberry Syrup.

May be made the same way as raspberry syrup (see No. 422). Select large fruit.

428. Barberry Syrup.

The method of making this is precisely the same as that for making Morello cherry syrup (see No. 425).

429. Capillaire (or Maidenhair) Syrup.

4 oz. of capillaire.

4 1/4 lbs. of sugar.

The best capillaire is found in America, and grows near ponds or running streams. The leaves are green, and grow double, the stalk long, and of the color of ripe plums. Be careful to obtain the genuine sort, whether foreign or native, whichever kind you require. Cut the capillaire into little pieces; then infuse them in boiling water, covering the pan over; add the sugar, and clarify with the whites of 4 eggs; if you are mixing in the above proportion boil to a " pearl" (see No. 13); then pour off through a strainer; when cool, add some orange-flower water; then bottle close. Ordinary syrup, with tincture of orange-flower in it, is often sold for the genuine article.

430. Lemon Syrup.

2 lbs. of sugar (or 2 pints of syrup).

1 pint of lemon juice.

Let the juice settle; clear off the thin skin, which forms on the top; then strain through a fine sieve or cloth; boil the syrup to the "little crack" (see No. 17); then pour in the lemon juice; place the pan on the fire, and boil to the "pearl" (see No. 13); skim as with raspberry (see No. 422), or mulberry syrup (see No. 426); bottle off when quite cool.

431. Orange Syrup.

Made the same way as lemon syrup (see No. 430).

432. Ginger Syrup.

2 oz. of ginger.

1 1/2 pint of water.

2 lbs. of sugar.

Boil together in a pan to the "small thread" (see No. 10), and strain through a hair sieve.

433. Pineapple Syrup.

Take a pineapple, cut the outside peel off, and pound it in a mortar; then strain it through a cloth; to pint of juice add 2 lbs. of sugar, and boil it to the "small thread" (see No. 10).

434. Violet Syrup.

1 lb. of violet flowers.

1 quart of water.

3 1/2 lbs. of sugar.

Remove the stalks, &c., and pour the water on the flowers hot; cover over, and let it remain a few hours in a warm place; then pass through a cloth; add the sugar, and boil to the "small thread" (see No. 10); the violet syrup sold in stores is often adulterated.

435. Grape Syrup.

1 1/2 pint of water.

½ do. sherry.

1/4 lb. of elder flowers.

3 lbs. of sugar.

Made the same way as violet syrup (see No. 434).

436. Raspberry Vinegar Syrup.

3 1/2 lbs. of sugar.

1 pint of raspberry juice.

2 pints of vinegar.

As in making raspberry syrup (see No. 422) white or red fruit may be used. White raspberries, however, require the best loaf sugar and white wine vinegar, so as not to discolor the syrup. Clean the raspberries; mash them in a pan, and put in a warm place, for a day or two, until they ferment; strain them, and pour in the vinegar ; strain again; add the sugar, and boil to the "pearl" (see No. 13). Another plan is to take whole raspberries (say 2 lbs., 1 1/2 pint of vinegar, and 2 lbs. of sugar), and put them in the vinegar, and stand the jar, well-covered, in a shady place for 10 days. At the expiration of this time filter the mixture; add the sugar, and place the jar in a pan of hot water, and boil gently. This mode preserves the finest qualities of the fruit, which are not partially lost by boiling, as in the previous method.

437. Coffee Syrup.

1 pint of coffee.

2 pints of syrup.

Make a strong decoction of Mocha coffee, very clear, to the amount of a pint; take 2 pints of syrup; boil it to a "ball" (see No. 16), and add the coffee; put it again on the fire; boil it to a "pearl" (see No. 13), and strain it through a cloth; bottle it when cold.

438. Wormwood Syrup.

1 ounce of wormwood.

1 lb. of sugar.

Make nearly a pint of the infusion of wormwood; add to it 1 lb. of loaf sugar; clarify it (see Nos. 6 and 7), and boil to a "pearl" (see No. 13); when cold, bottle it.

439. Marsh-Mallow Syrup.

Take 2 ounces of marsh-mallow roots; cut them into small pieces; bruise them in a mortar, and boil the mallows in 1 1/2 pint of water, till reduced to a pint; then clear it, and add 1 lb. of sugar, finishing it in the same way as capillaire (see No. 429).

440. Syrup of Pinks.

½ lb. of pinks.

1 lb. of sugar.

Pick off all the green parts from half a pound of pinks; put the flowers in a mortar, and pound them with a pint of boiling water; strain the decoction through a cloth; clarify 1 lb. of loaf sugar (see No. 6); boil it to a "ball" (see No. 16), and add it to the decoction; put it again on the fire, and boil it to a " pearl" (see No. 13). This syrup may also be made without pounding the flowers, only boiling them with the sugar; when done, skim it, and strain it through a cloth. The dark-red velvety single-pink is the best for syrup.

441. Baths.

Every liqueur made by infusions is called ratafia; that is, when the spirit is made to imbibe thoroughly the aromatic flavor and color of the fruit steeped in it; when this has taken place the liquor is drawn off, and sugar added to it; it is then filtered and bottled.

442. Ratafia of Cherries.

Wild cherries, 10 lbs.; Morello cherries, 10 lbs. ; cinnamon, 2 drachms; mace, 2 drachms; brandy, 8 pints; strawberries, 2 lbs.; raspberries, 2 lbs.; corianders, 4 ounces, and 4 ounces of sugar to every pint of juice. Crush the fruit; strain the juice through a sieve, and pound the stones, coriander, cinnamon, and mace, separately, and infuse the whole in a jar. To every pint of juice add 4 ounces of sugar; let it steep for a month; filter it, and bottle for

443. Another Ratafia of Cherries.

Juice of Morello cherries, 15 pints; peach leaves, 1 lb.; brandy, 14 pints; cinnamon, 3 drachms; cloves, 1 drachm; sugar, 8 lbs. Crush and strain through a sieve the pulp of your cherries; pound the stones; put them altogether in a pan on the fire, and give them one boil; when cold measure the juice; and when you have 15 pints add your peach leaves, cinnamon, and cloves, which must have been previously bruised in a mortar, the sugar and brandy being added; put the whole into a jar; leave it for a month; draw it off, and bottle it.

444. Ratafia from four Fruits.

Morello cherries, 8 lbs.; wild cherries, 6 lbs.; raspberries, 4 lbs.; red currants, 8 lbs.; black currants, 4 lbs.; mace, 1 drachm; cloves, 1 drachm, and 4 ounces of sugar to every pint of juice. Proceed in the same manner as for cherries.

445. Ratafia of Black Currants.

Black currants, 4 lbs.; black currant leaves, 1 lb.; Morello cherries, 2 lbs.; cloves, 1 drachm; brandy, 10 pints; sugar, 10 lbs. Steep them as above.

446. Badiane.

Brandy, 3 pints; water, 3 pints; bitter almonds, 1 lb.; sugar, 1 lb.; 1 lemon peel, rasped; six cloves; cinnamon, 1 ounce. Break up the whole; put it into a jar with the lemon peel, the sugar being melted in 3 pints of water; infuse for a month; strain it through a flannel bag, and then filter the liquor and bottle it.

447. Ratafia of Orange.

6 China oranges, 2 lbs. of sugar, 4 pints of brandy, and 1 pint of water; peel 6 fine oranges; infuse the rind in the brandy for 15 days; melt your sugar in the cold water, and strain and filter it as above.

448. Ratafia of Raspberries.

Raspberries, 10 lbs.; sugar, 4.lbs.; brandy, 10 pints; cinnamon, 2 drachms; cloves, 1 drachm; infuse the articles for 15 days; stir the mixture every day; strain through a bag and filter it.

449. Ratafia of Currants.

Currants, 10 lbs.; brandy, 10 pints; sugar, 4 lbs; cinnamon, 2 drachms; cloves, 2 drachms, and proceed as for raspberries.

450. Ratafia of Mulberries.

Mulberries, 10 lbs.; brandy, 10 pints; sugar, 4 lbs.; mace, 2 drachms. Proceed as before.

451. Ratafia of Orange-flowers.

Brandy, 3 pints; water, 2 pints; orange-flowers, 1 lb.; and sugar, 1 lb. Put the whole in a jar well stopped; place it in a bath, almost boiling hot, for a day; the next day filter and bottle it.

452. Vespitro.

Brandy, 2 pints; anise-seed, 1 ounce; 2 lemons; sugar, 1 lb.; corianders, 2 ounces; fennel, 1 ounce; angelica, 2 drachms. Break up these ingredients, and put them in a jar with 2 pints of brandy; peel the 2 lemons, which you must add to the mixture, and squeeze in the juice; break the sugar; dissolve it in water, and put it into the jar; let it stand for a fortnight; then strain it through a flannel bag; filter and bottle it.

453. Yellow Escubac.

1 ounce of saffron; 1 ounce of Damascus raisins; 1 ounce of cinnamon; 3 lbs. of sugar: 1 ounce of liquorice; 1 ounce of coriander ; 3 pints of brandy; 2 pints of water. Pound these ingredients, and dissolve the sugar in 2 pints of water; put the whole in a jar to infuse for a month, taking care to stir it up every second day, or the third at farthest.

454. Ratafia of Green Walnut Shells.

200 walnuts, 10 pints of brandy, 4 lbs. of sugar, 1 drachm of nutmeg, 1 drachm of cloves. Choose 200 walnuts so young that a pin may easily go through them; pound them in a mortar, and infuse them in the brandy, with the nutmeg and cloves, for a month; after that time strain the mixture through a flannel bag, filter, and bottle it.

455. Angelica Ratafia.

4 ounces of angelica-seed, 2 ounces of the roots of angelica, 10 pints of brandy, 1 drachm of cloves, 1 drachm of cinnamon, 4 pounds of sugar. Pound the ingredients coarsely; dissolve the sugar in water, and add it to the mixture; infuse it in the brandy for a month; strain it through a bag and filter it.

456. Ratafia of Red Pinks.

3 lbs. of pinks, 10 pints of brandy, 4 lbs. of sugar, 1 drachm of cloves, 1 drachm of cinnamon. Pick off the green from your pinks, pound the leaves, and infuse them for a month in the brandy, with the cloves and cinnamon; after this draw off the liquor and filter it.

457. Balm of Molucca.

1 drachm of mace, shreded. 1 ounce of cloves, bruised. 1 gallon of clean spirit (22 under proof). Macerate for a week in a well-corked demijohn or jar, frequently shaking (see No. 5); color with coloring (see No. 88), and add lbs. of lump sugar dissolved in a gallon of pure soft water.

458. Tears of the Widow of Malabar.

Same as Balm of Molucca, but employing 1 drachm of mace (shreded), ½ an ounce of cloves (bruised), and a teaspoonful of the essence of vanilla for flavoring. Some add ¼ of a pint of orange-flower water. It is slightly colored with coloring. (See No. 88.)

459. Sighs of Love.

6 lbs. of sugar, and pure soft water sufficient to produce a gallon of syrup (see Nos. 7 and 421), to which add 1 pint of rose water and 7 pints of proof spirit; color pale pink (see No. 93). A drop or two (not more) of the essence of ambergris or vanilla improves it. This is a pleasant cordial.

460. Delight of the Mandarins.

1 gallon of spirit (22 under proof).

½ do. pure soft water.

4 1/2 lbs. of white sugar (crushed small).

½ ounce of anisum Chinse, bruised.

½ do. ambrette or musk seed, bruised.

¼ do. safflower.

Macerate in a carboy or stone jar capable of holding double the quantity (see No. 5), and agitate well every day for 2 weeks.

461. Elephant's Milk.

2 ounces of gum benzoin.

1 pint of rectified spirits of wine.

Dissolve and add 2 1/2 pints of boiling water; agitate for 5 minutes in a strong corked bottle, and when cold strain and add 1 1/2 lb. of lump sugar.

462. Vanilla Milk.

12 drops of essence of vanilla.

1 ounce of lump sugar.

Pulverize and add gradually 1 pint of new milk.

463. Yankee Punch.

Macerate 3 ounces of sliced pineapple, 6 grains of vanilla, 1 grain of ambergris (rubbed with a little sugar) in 1 pint of the strongest pale brandy for a few hours, being careful to shake it frequently during that time (see No. 5); then strain through a jelly bag, squeezing the bag so as to get all the liquid, and add of lemon juice 1 pint, 1 bottle of lemon syrup, 1 bottle of claret or port wine, and 1/2 lb. of sugar dissolved in 1 1/2 pint of boiling water.